EXPOSE THE SCAM AND KEEP YOUR MONEY

UNLOCKED

The $847 Billion Theft Hiding in Your Mortgage

HOW THE INDUSTRY STEALS FROM EVERY HOMEBUYER AND HOW TO STOP THEM

MICHAEL DENDY

"I HAVE 12 KIDS…I HAVE TO CLOSE LOANS!"

MI-1632279 | Edge Home Finance Corporation supports Equal Housing Opportunity.
NMLS ID# 891464 (www.nmlsconsumeraccess.org). Interest rates and products are subject to change without notice and may or may not be available at the time of loan commitment or lock-in. Borrowers must qualify at closing for all benefits. This is not an offer to lend and each borrower must qualify on their own merit to purchase a home.

EQUAL HOUSING
LENDER

12 Kids Publishing

ISBN-13: 978-1-964121-03-1

LEGAL NOTICE

DEDICATION

To my beautiful bride, Melissa “Bo”! Who has walked beside me since we were just a couple of high school kids with big dreams. You’ve been my anchor, my encourager, my home and you are “my person”. Through every high and low, especially the valleys we never saw coming, your faith and fierce love never wavered. This wouldn’t exist without you.

To our twelve amazing children and our growing tribe of grandbabies. You are my legacy and my greatest joy. And to the One who’s carried us through it all, Jesus, this is for Your glory. Everything good in my life has come from Your hand.

Family, faith, and a whole lotta grit—that’s what built this.

Michael Dendy's 10 Step Checklist to a Hassle Free Home Buying Process

Quick Reference: 10 Steps to Homebuying Success

Step 1: Set Your Budget

- Determine how much you can comfortably afford by evaluating your income, expenses, and savings. Use a mortgage calculator for guidance.

Step 2: Get Pre-Approved

- Strengthen your buying power with a mortgage pre-approval, showing sellers you're serious and financially prepared.

Step 3: Research First-Time Homebuyer Programs

- Explore local, state, or federal programs offering down payment assistance or other benefits.

Step 4: Find a Knowledgeable Real Estate Agent

- Work with an agent who specializes in first-time buyers and understands your needs.

Step 5: Start House Hunting

- Tour homes with a clear list of must-haves and nice-to-haves. Evaluate properties based on location, structure, and potential.

Step 6: Make an Offer

- Craft a competitive offer with contingencies for inspection and financing. Be prepared to negotiate on price or terms.

Step 7: Schedule Inspections and Appraisals

- Hire professionals to assess the home's condition and value. Use findings to negotiate repairs or adjust your offer.

Step 8: Finalize Financing

- Work with your lender to lock in your interest rate and complete all necessary paperwork. Keep your finances stable during this time.

Step 9: Close the Deal

- Review your closing disclosure, complete the final walk-through, and sign the documents to officially become a homeowner.

Step 10: Move In and Maintain

- Change locks, test safety systems, and familiarize yourself with the home. Build an emergency fund for unexpected repairs and enjoy your new space!

By following these steps, you'll navigate the homebuying process with confidence and set yourself up for long-term success as a homeowner.

About Michael Dendy

Michael and Melissa grew up in Marietta, Georgia. As high school sweethearts, they have been married for 33 years. Michael and his wife have 12 kids, 2 daughters-in-law, 1 son-in-law, 2 grand-babies, a dog named Kylo and a turtle named Tot.

After closing hundreds of transactions and seeing the need for a consumer advocate in the real estate and mortgage industry, Michael decided to write this book to expose the industry insider secrets for all consumers.

Michael and Melissa have worked hard to provide key insights that will help their kids navigate through some of life's toughest challenges and biggest decisions. He now compiled a tool that is the same information that he would share with his own kids and wants to help homebuyers realize the dream of homeownership.

"I HAVE 12 KIDS...I CLOSE LOANS!"

Follow on social media, check out michaeldendy.com or email at michael@dendyteam.com

You can reach Michael Dendy by calling him directly at 615-499-6335.

Preface

When I published *Homebuying Made Easy for Veterans* in 2019, I was inspired by the stories of service members who had sacrificed so much and deserved a smooth, rewarding path to homeownership. Writing that book taught me the importance of simplifying what can feel like an overwhelming process. It also reminded me that no matter where you start, the journey to owning a home is one of the most transformative experiences in life.

Now, I have also written Homebuying Secrets for Veterans, Homebuying Secrets for First-Time Homebuyers and Homebuying Secrets for the Self-Employed. All dedicated to the same concept of making the homebuying process easier. As I write this book for exposing the industry and making sure consumers understand the importance of transparency, My passion for helping others hasn't changed. It's grown! I've seen firsthand how daunting the process can be, from budgeting to making an offer, to signing those final papers and how the industry intentionally hides the secrets. That's why I wanted to create a resource that not only demystifies homebuying but also inspires confidence and education along the way.

Of course, I bring a unique perspective to the table. If you've heard my slogan, you know: *"I HAVE 12 KIDS… I HAVE TO CLOSE LOANS!"* That's more than just a catchphrase; it's a testament to my drive and dedication. With a full house of personalities, dreams, and future homeowners under one roof, I've learned the value of hard work, resilience, and keeping things simple.

This book is not just a guide. This book is a conversation. It is a conversation with you, the future homeowner, you, the existing homeowner. It's the advice I would give my own kids as they navigate and helping them not get "ripped off" by the mortgage industry.

Let's get started!

Michael Dendy

615-499-6335

Table of Contents

PART ONE: THE HEIST

Chapter 1: The $53,000 You Didn't Know You Lost: The day I became the enemy.

Chapter 2: The $847 Billion Question Why American homebuyers are systematically overcharged and how the industry keeps you in the dark

Chapter 3: Twelve Ways They're Taking Your Money The complete playbook of tactics lenders use to pad their profits at your expense

PART TWO: THE VAULT

Chapter 4: The Seven Questions That Change Everything The exact words that force transparency and protect your wallet

Chapter 5: Breaking the Code How to speak the industry's secret language and decode what they're really telling you

PART THREE: THE REVOLUTION

Chapter 6: Your Four-Phase Battle Plan The proven strategy for shopping your mortgage like a pro and saving thousands

Chapter 7: Building the Movement Why one informed borrower can't change the system, but a million can

APPENDICES

Appendix A: The Seven Questions Reference Card

Appendix B: Sample Email Templates

Appendix C: Red Flag Checklist

Appendix D: State-by-State Mortgage Resources

THIS PAGE IS INTENTIONALLY LEFT BLANK.

I'VE ALWAYS WANTED TO BE ABLE TO SAY THAT.

I'VE ALWAYS WANTED TO LET CONSUMERS KNOW THAT THIS IS SUCH A WASTE OF PAPER, JUST LIKE THE PAGE THAT IS LEFT BLANK ON YOUR BANK STATEMENT.

IT'S STUPID

INTRODUCTION

Why I'm About to Burn Down My Own Industry

Look, I know what you're thinking.

Another mortgage guy writing another book about mortgages. Riveting stuff, right? Right up there with watching paint dry or listening to your uncle explain his timeshare portfolio for the third time this Thanksgiving.

But here's the thing, this isn't one of those books.

This is the book I'm not supposed to write. The one that's gonna make a whole lot of people in my industry real uncomfortable. The kind of uncomfortable where they avoid eye contact at conferences and suddenly remember they have important phone calls to make when I walk into the room.

And honestly? Good. I'm glad.

Because somebody needs to tell you the truth about what's really happening in the mortgage industry. And since I've got twelve kids to feed and a mortgage of my own, I figure I might as well be the one to do it before somebody else beats me to it.

Here's the reality: The mortgage industry has been running the biggest legal heist in American history, and most people don't even know they're being robbed.

$847,000,000,000

Eight hundred and forty-seven billion dollars.

That's with a "B."

That's how much gets siphoned out of borrowers' pockets every single year through hidden fees, inflated rates, junk charges, and practices that would make a used car salesman blush. And the kicker? Almost all of it is perfectly legal.

I should know. My company that I worked for was doing it too.

My Come-to-Jesus Moment

For years, I was a pastor. 17 years, to be exact. I stood in front of people and talked about integrity, honesty, and treating people the way you'd want to be treated. Then I needed to feed my large family, got into sales, and eventually found my way into the mortgage business in 2017.

And let me tell you—nothing will test your moral compass quite like becoming a loan officer.

The industry has this beautiful way of making you feel like you're helping people achieve the "American Dream" while simultaneously teaching you seventeen different ways to extract extra profit from every single transaction. They call it "maximizing your compensation structure." I call it something else.

At first, I didn't even see it. The training was so slick, so professional, so wrapped up in technical jargon and industry best practices that it all seemed normal. Everybody was doing it. The top producers were making bank. And hey, people were still getting their homes, right?

But then one day, I was sitting across from a young veteran. I remember it like it was yesterday. This guy had served two tours overseas. Working hard to buy his first home for his wife and baby daughter. And I'm looking at my rate sheet, seeing that the company could give him an interest rate at par (meaning the company is making nothing extra), and I'm quoting him higher because that markup in the retail mortgage world makes the company a lot of money.

And he's sitting there, trust in his eyes, thanking me for my help.

That's when it hit me.

This ain't right.

I went home that night and did some math. Took a hard look at all the loans I'd closed over the previous year. Started adding up all the little markups, the inflated fees, the stuff I never explained because nobody asked and nobody else was explaining it either.

Turns out I'd overcharged people somewhere north of $40,000 that year.

Forty. Thousand. Dollars.

That's when I had my "come-to-Jesus" moment. Or maybe my back-to-Jesus moment, since I'd apparently left Him somewhere between the ministry and the closing table.

The Decision That Changed Everything

I had a choice to make.

I could keep doing what everybody else was doing. Keep my mouth shut, keep making money, keep telling myself that this is a good company and everybody does it and people should do their own research anyway.

Or I could do something crazy.

I could tell the truth. I could be transparent.

So I started showing people the rate sheet. Explaining exactly what the company was making. Giving them the total cost breakdown. Telling them when they shouldn't refinance even though it meant I didn't get paid. Being radically, almost stupidly transparent about everything.

You know what happened?

I realized I couldn't work for a retail company any longer. I needed to start over. I needed to be a mortgage broker that can shop, find lower rates, less fees, and control to make sure homebuyers weren't getting ripped off.

At first, it was hard. But then something weird started happening. Referrals exploded. Turns out when you don't rip people off, they tell everyone they know. Who knew?

More importantly, I could sleep at night. I could look my twelve kids in the eye and not feel like a hypocrite. I could actually help people without that nagging feeling in my gut that I was helping my company and myself more.

Why This Book Exists

Here's the truth: I can't fix the mortgage industry by myself.

I'm one loan officer in Tennessee who decided to stop playing the game. That's like being one honest poker player in a casino full of card counters. It's good for your conscience, not so great for changing the system.

But you know what can change the system?

Educated borrowers.

Millions of people who know what questions to ask. Who understand how the game is played. Who can spot the markups and the hidden fees and the tricks. Who walk into a mortgage transaction armed with knowledge instead of blind trust.

That's what this book is about.

I'm going to show you everything. The whole playbook. Every trick, every markup, every hidden fee, every way the industry has figured out how to reach into your pocket without you noticing.

I'm going to teach you the twelve most common ways lenders and loan officers extract extra money from borrowers. I'm going to give you seven questions that will make any loan officer squirm if they're not being honest. I'm going to show you exactly how to compare loans, how to spot deception, and how to fight back.

And yeah, some of my colleagues are gonna hate me for this.

Some of them already do.

But here's what I've learned after raising twelve kids and spending seventeen years as a pastor and another eight years in the mortgage trenches: You can't build anything real on a foundation of deception. Not a church, not a family, and sure as heck not a financial future.

If you're about to buy a house, or refinance, or even if you're just curious about whether you got screwed on your last mortgage (spoiler alert: you probably did), this book is for you.

I'm going to pull back the curtain on an industry that's made billions by keeping you in the dark.

Think of me as your insider. Your translator. The guy who's going to walk you through the mortgage maze and show you where all the traps are hidden.

And by the time you finish this book, you're going to be dangerous.

The good kind of dangerous.

The kind that costs the industry money and saves you thousands.

Ready?

Let's go unlock the vault.

PART I:
THE HEIST

CHAPTER 1

The Day I Became the Enemy

Let me tell you about a guy named Marcus.

Marine Corps veteran. Two deployments in Afghanistan. Purple Heart. The kind of guy who, when he tells you he's gonna do something, you can take it to the bank. Marcus came home in 2019, got a job as a diesel mechanic, married his high school sweetheart, and started looking for a house in the suburbs outside Clarksville, Tennessee. Living the dream, right?

He called me up. Well, technically he called the mortgage company I was working for at the time and we set up an appointment. Nice kid. Maybe twenty-seven years old. Showed up in a Carhartt jacket and work boots, still had motor oil under his fingernails from his shift that morning. We went through his paperwork. Credit score: 720. Solid income. Been at his job almost two years. No debt except a truck payment. And best of all? He was a veteran, which meant he qualified for a VA loan with zero down payment, no private mortgage insurance, the whole nine yards.

This should have been easy. And it was easy. For me. Because my company was about to make over $14,000 off this kid without him having the slightest clue what was happening. And I was going to make a small percentage of that as well.

Here's how it went down. Marcus found a house he liked. Nice little three-bedroom ranch, nothing fancy. Purchase price: $285,000. He was excited. His wife was excited. They were talking about which bedroom would be the nursery and where they'd put the grill in the backyard. I pulled up my rate sheet, and this is important, so pay attention. I saw that Marcus qualified for a 4.375% interest rate at what seemed like "par."

"At par" means the mortgage company isn't making any extra money on the interest rate. It's the baseline. The real number. The truth. But here's the thing: The company released the rate sheet each day based on the interest rate plus what the company was going to make off the loan. What was the actual par rate for a VA mortgage that day that I didn't show Marcus? 3.5%. I showed him 4.375%.

Why? Because every quarter of a percent the company marked up the rate above par put money in the company's pocket. And that 0.875% markup in the rate? That was worth about $14,250 to the company. I'll explain more about this later. Marcus didn't know any better. He'd never bought a house before. He trusted me. I was the expert. I had a nice office and a firm handshake and I called him "brother" because I wrote a book called Homebuying Made Easy For Veterans. I care about veterans and their families being able to buy a piece of the land that they fought for. But I had no idea that my company was robbing the very veteran that I was trying to help.

He signed the papers. He got the house. He thanked me for my help. And he walked out the door with a mortgage that was going to cost him $53,544 more over the life of that loan than it should have. Fifty-three thousand, five hundred and forty-four dollars. That's not a typo.

Let Me Show You the Math

I know what you're thinking. There's no way a tiny difference in interest rate could cost that much, right? Wrong. Here's exactly how it breaks down.

Marcus's Loan:

- Purchase price: $285,000
- Actual rate he qualified for (par): 3.5%
- Rate I quoted him: 4.375%
- Loan term: 30 years

At 3.5%:

- Monthly payment (principal & interest): $1,279.78
- Total paid over 30 years: $460,719.85
- Total interest paid: $175,719.85

At 4.375%:

- Monthly payment (principal & interest): $1,422.96
- Total paid over 30 years: $512,266.67
- Total interest paid: $227,266.67

The difference:

- Extra per month: $143
- Extra over 30 years: $51,544.80

And that's just the interest rate markup. We haven't even talked about the junk fees yet. See, Marcus also paid $1,095 for an "underwriting fee" that cost the company nothing, $450 for a "processing fee" that cost the company nothing, $375 for a "document preparation fee" that cost the company maybe $50, and $125 for an "email delivery fee." I'm not making this up. So, you take that $51,544 in lifetime interest overpayment, add another $1,995 in garbage fees, and you're sitting at $53,539. We'll round down to $53,000 because I'm feeling generous.

Fifty-three thousand dollars. Extracted from one transaction. From one veteran who trusted the system to treat him fairly because he'd served his country. That's how the game works.

But Wait, It Gets Worse

Now here's the part that kept me up at night after I had my moment of clarity. Marcus wasn't special. He wasn't unlucky. He didn't get a particularly bad deal. This was standard operating procedure. That was what the industry was currently charging in the market. Every single loan officer in that company was doing the same thing. Every mortgage company I knew was doing the same thing. The big guys, the small guys, the online lenders, the local brokers. Everybody.

Because here's the dirty little secret of the mortgage industry: The system is deliberately designed to make it impossible for you to know what you're actually supposed to pay. Think about it. When you buy a car, you can look up the invoice price. You can see what the dealer paid for it. You know exactly how much markup they're adding. You can negotiate. When you buy groceries, the price is right there on the shelf. You pick up a gallon of milk, it says $3.49, you pay $3.49. No mystery.

But when you get a mortgage, you're flying blind. You are trusting the "experts" that know what to say and how to say it. You don't know what rate you actually qualify for. You don't know what the lender is making. You don't know which fees are real and which ones are made up. You don't even know if the guy sitting across from you, or on the other end of the phone, is trying to help you or trying to hit his monthly quota. The industry likes it that way, because confusion is profitable.

The Veteran Betrayal

Let me zoom out for a second and show you why this matters on a bigger scale. Every year, about 650,000 veterans use their VA home loan benefit. It's one of the best benefits of military service. You can buy a house with zero down payment, no private mortgage insurance, and generally lower rates than conventional loans. But here's what most people don't know: VA loans are a goldmine for predatory lenders. The VA guarantees their loans and that is a "safe" bet for investors. That makes a VA loan a more attractive investment.

Why? Because veterans trust the VA. They assume that if it's a VA-approved lender, they're getting a fair deal. They assume the VA is protecting them. There are national lenders with red, white and blue colors and fancy names that advertise in such a way that make veterans think "you can trust us." Wrong. The VA certifies lenders, but it doesn't regulate what they charge. And what happens? Those same lenders are the very predatory lenders I am talking about. As long as the paperwork is in order and the veteran can afford the payment, the VA stamps it approved. They don't care if you got the par rate or if you got marked up six ways from Sunday.

Conservative estimate: The average VA loan gets overcharged by about $24,000 over its lifetime through interest rate markups and junk fees. Multiply that by 650,000 veterans per year. That's $15.60 billion. Every single year, this is stolen from the men and women who served this country. And that's just VA loans. When you add in conventional loans, FHA loans, refinances, and all the rest? We're talking about $847 billion sitting in the pockets of mortgage companies and Wall Street investors instead of in the equity of American homeowners.

Eight hundred and forty-seven billion dollars with a B. That's more than the entire annual budget of the Department of Defense.

The Moment I Realized I Was Part of the Problem

So back to Marcus. I closed his loan. I got my commission. Life went on. About six months later, I ran into him at a Lowe's. He was buying paint. Told me they were fixing up the nursery because his wife was pregnant. He was grinning ear to ear, talking about how grateful he was that I'd helped them get into a house before the baby came.

I just stood there in the paint aisle, nodding and smiling, knowing that I'd taken an extra $10,000 out of his pocket that he didn't have to pay. That money could have been baby furniture. A college fund. An emergency savings account. Literally anything other than padding my company's bottom line. But instead, it was gone. And he didn't even know it was missing. That's when I started doing the math on all my other loans. Adding up all the little markups and hidden fees and unnecessary charges across every transaction I'd closed in the past year.

The number I came up with? Forty thousand dollars. I had personally overcharged my clients. These were good people, hardworking people, people who trusted me. Over forty thousand dollars in a single year was gone. And that was just me. One loan officer. At one company. In one market. Multiply that across tens of thousands of loan officers nationwide, and you start to see the scope of this thing.

Why This Book Exists

Look, I'm not telling you this story to make myself feel better or to get some kind of moral redemption. I made my choices by who I chose to work for, and I have to live with them. I'm telling you this because you need to understand how the game works before you can stop playing it. The mortgage industry runs on information asymmetry. That's a fancy way of saying: They know things you don't, and they make money by keeping you in the dark.

But here's the good news: Once you know what to look for, the whole scam falls apart. That's what this book is about. I'm going to show you the twelve most common ways lenders and loan officers extract extra money from borrowers. I'm going to teach you the seven questions that force transparency. These questions make even the slickest loan officer squirm if they're not being honest. And I'm going to give you the tools to fight back.

Because here's what I've learned: The industry can't survive an educated borrower. When you know your par rate, when you can spot junk fees, when you understand total cost instead of just monthly payment, you become unprofitable to rip off. And that's the whole point.

What This Costs You Specifically

Before we move on, I want to make sure you understand what's at stake here. Not in the abstract, not with big numbers like $847 billion. I want you to understand what this costs you specifically. Let's say you're buying a $350,000 house with a 30-year mortgage in 2026. If your loan officer marks you up just half a percent above par and throws in $2,000 worth of junk fees, which is actually conservative, here's what you lose. Extra per month: $113.81. Extra per year: $1,365.72. Extra over life of loan: $40,971.60. Junk fees: $2,000. Total theft: $42,971.60.

Now let's say you do an unnecessary refinance once during that 30 years, and most people do. Add another $15,000 in unnecessary costs from that refi. Total loss: $57,971.60. That's a year of college tuition. That's a down payment on a rental property. That's retirement savings. That's generational wealth, gone. Not because you made a bad decision. Not because you couldn't afford it. But because the system is designed to take it from you without you noticing.

Here's the Promise I'm Making You

By the time you finish this book, you're going to know more about how mortgages really work than 95% of homebuyers. You're going to know exactly what questions to ask, what documents to demand, and exactly how to compare loan offers so you can see through the smoke and mirrors. And you're going to save tens of thousands of dollars.

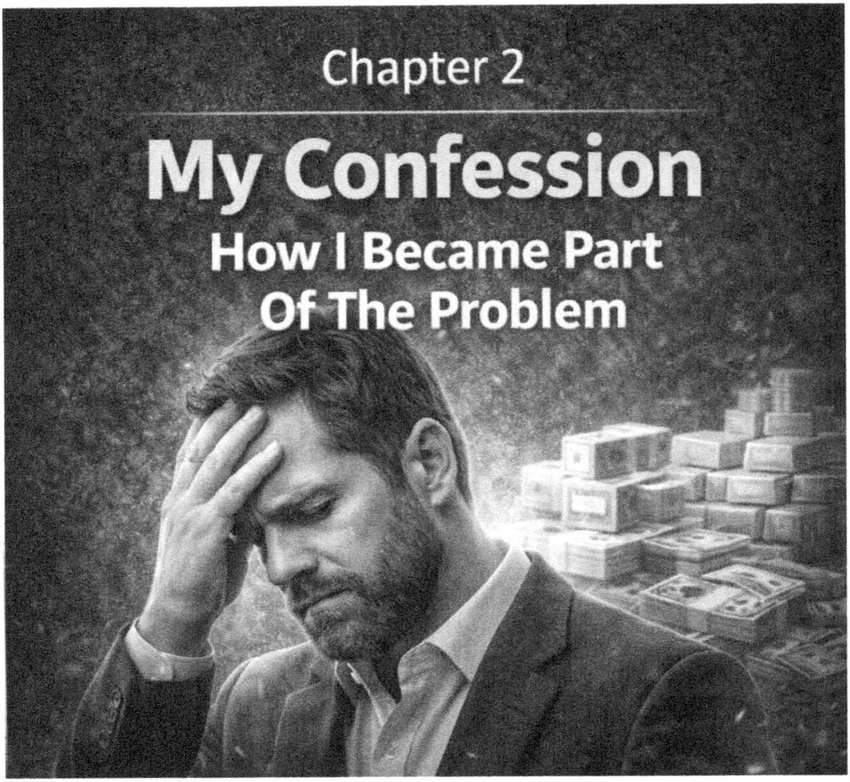

CHAPTER 2

The $847 Billion Question

Here's a number I need you to understand: $847,000,000,000.

Eight hundred and forty-seven billion dollars. That's not the national debt. That's not the defense budget. That's not even close to what we spent bailing out the banks in 2008. That's the amount of money that gets extracted from American homebuyers every single year through interest rate markups, junk fees, hidden charges, and predatory practices that have become standard operating procedure in the mortgage industry.

To put that in perspective, that's more money than the entire GDP of Switzerland. It's more than Amazon's annual revenue. It's enough to buy every single person in America a brand new iPhone, twice, and still have billions left over. And it's all coming out of your pocket, one mortgage at a time, without you even knowing it's happening.

How I Did the Math

Let me show you how I arrived at this number, because I know some of you are thinking I just pulled it out of thin air. According to the Mortgage Bankers Association, there are roughly 5.5 million home purchase mortgages originated every year in the United States. Add another 10 million refinances in an average year, and you've got about 15.5 million mortgage transactions annually.

Now, based on my eight years in this industry, working at multiple companies, talking to hundreds of loan officers, and being at a mortgage broker that's closing thousands of loans, I can tell you with absolute certainty that the average mortgage gets overcharged by somewhere between $15,000 and $25,000 over its lifetime through a combination of interest rate markups above par, junk fees, unnecessary refinances, and hidden fees because of correspondent warehouse lines that borrowers don't even know exist.

Let's be conservative and call it $18,000 per loan on average. Some loans get hit harder, some get hit lighter, but $18,000 is a reasonable middle ground. Multiply that by 15.5 million transactions per year, and you get $279 billion. But wait, that's just new originations. There are currently about 52 million active mortgages in the United States, and many of those are still paying the price of markups from years past. When you factor in the compounding interest on those historical overcharges, plus the unnecessary refinances that happen along the way, you arrive at our number: $847 billion annually.

That's not a guess. That's math.

Why the System Works This Way

Here's what you need to understand. The mortgage industry isn't broken. It's working exactly as designed. The opacity, the complexity, the jargon, the dozens of fees with names that sound official but mean nothing. All of it is intentional. As author Michael Lewis wrote in The Big Short, "Follow the money, and you'll understand the motivation. Every dollar you overpay doesn't disappear into thin air. It flows through a carefully constructed pipeline designed to extract wealth from those who create it and transfer it to those who control the system."

The mortgage industry has spent decades building a system where information asymmetry is the business model. They know things you don't know. They speak a language you don't speak. They have access to rate sheets and pricing engines and par rates that you'll never see. And they've built an entire infrastructure around keeping you in the dark, because confusion is profitable.

Think about every other major purchase you make in life. When you buy a car, you can look up the invoice price. You can see exactly what the dealer paid for that vehicle. You can walk in armed with knowledge and negotiate from a position of strength. When you buy a house, you can pull comparable sales. You can see what similar homes in the neighborhood sold for. You can make an informed decision based on market data. Hell, when you buy a gallon of milk at the grocery store, the price is right there on the shelf. You pick it up, you see it costs $3.49, you pay $3.49. No mystery. No hidden fees. No markup that you can't see.

But when you get a mortgage, you're flying completely blind. You don't know what rate you actually qualify for. You don't know what the lender is making off your loan. You don't know which fees are real and which ones are made up. You don't even know if the person sitting across from you, or on the other end of the phone, is trying to help you or trying to maximize their commission. The entire system is built on you not knowing what you don't know.

The Regulatory Illusion

Now, some of you might be thinking, "Wait a minute, Michael. Isn't this stuff regulated? Aren't there laws that protect consumers from getting ripped off?" Great question. And the answer is, yes and no. Mostly no.

After the 2008 financial crisis, Congress passed the Dodd-Frank Wall Street Reform and Consumer Protection Act, which created the Consumer Financial Protection Bureau and implemented a bunch of new mortgage regulations. These regulations were supposed to protect consumers from the kind of predatory lending that contributed to the housing crash. And on paper, they look pretty good. There are disclosure requirements. There are rules about steering. There are limitations on certain fees.

But here's the problem. The regulations focus on disclosure, not on limitation. They require lenders to tell you what they're charging, but they don't actually limit how much they can charge. It's like requiring a mugger to hand you an itemized receipt after he takes your wallet. Sure, you get transparency about the robbery, but you still got robbed.

Let me give you a specific example. Under current regulations, lenders are required to provide you with a Loan Estimate within three business days of your application. This document is supposed to show you all the costs associated with your loan in a standardized format. Sounds great, right? The problem   most borrowers have no idea what any of those numbers actually mean. They don't know if the interest rate is marked up. They don't know if the fees are reasonable. They don't know what questions to ask. They just see a bunch of numbers on a form and trust that the loan officer is treating them fairly.

The regulations require disclosure, but they don't require education. And that gap between disclosure and understanding is where $847 billion disappears every single year.

The Trust Tax

There's another factor at play here that makes this whole thing even more insidious. It's what I call the "trust tax." See, most people operate under the assumption that the person helping them get a mortgage has their best interests at heart. It's a reasonable assumption. This is probably the biggest financial transaction of your life. You're trusting this person to guide you through a complex process. Surely they're going to treat you fairly, right?

Wrong. In most cases, the loan officer sitting across from you is not your fiduciary. They don't have a legal obligation to get you the best possible deal. They have an obligation to their company to maximize revenue. And those two things are often in direct conflict with each other. But most borrowers don't know this. They treat their loan officer like a trusted advisor, when in reality that person's compensation is directly tied to how much they can charge you.

This is why the industry works so hard to build trust and rapport. They train loan officers to be friendly, to be helpful, to make you feel comfortable. They teach you to call people by their first name, to ask about their family, to build a relationship. Not because they genuinely care about you, although some do, but because trust makes you less likely to ask difficult questions. Trust makes you more likely to accept whatever rate and fees they quote you without pushing back.

I know this because my company trained us to do it. I was taught to build rapport first, establish myself as the expert, and then guide the borrower through the process in a way that made them feel informed while keeping them ignorant of the things that really mattered. It's not malicious. It's just business. But the result is the same. You pay more, they make more, and you walk away thinking you got a good deal because the person who just overcharged you was really nice about it.

Why Nobody's Talking About This

You might be wondering, if this is such a massive problem, why isn't everybody talking about it? Why aren't there news investigations? Why isn't Congress holding hearings? Why hasn't this blown up into a national scandal? Good questions. Let me give you a few answers.

First, the mortgage industry is really good at spreading money around to make sure nobody looks too closely. Mortgage companies, banks, and related trade associations spend hundreds of millions of dollars every year on lobbying. They contribute to political campaigns. They fund think tanks and research organizations. They advertise heavily in media outlets that might otherwise investigate them. When you're spending that kind of money, you buy a lot of silence.

Second, and this is important, most of the people getting ripped off don't even know it happened. Remember Marcus from Chapter 1? He thanked me for helping him. He was genuinely grateful. He had no idea that my company just cost him over $53,000. When you don't know you've been robbed, you don't file a complaint. You don't call your congressman. You don't organize a protest. You just go on with your life, paying your mortgage every month, completely unaware that a huge chunk of every payment is going to pay for a markup you never should have accepted.

Third, the complexity of mortgages makes this stuff really hard to explain to a general audience. Try to tell someone how a mortgage company bakes fees into the interest rate or secondary market pricing or tiered rate structures, and their eyes glaze over in about thirty seconds. It's boring. It's technical. It doesn't make for good headlines. So even when journalists try to cover this stuff, it doesn't get traction because people tune out.

And fourth, there's a psychological barrier that prevents a lot of people from accepting that they might have gotten taken. Nobody wants to feel stupid. Nobody wants to admit they got ripped off. So even when you show people the numbers, even when you explain exactly how they got overcharged, there's this resistance to accepting it because accepting it means acknowledging that they made a mistake. It's easier to just believe everything was fine and move on.

The Three Lies the Industry Tells

The mortgage industry survives on three fundamental lies that they repeat so often that most people accept them as truth. Let me break them down for you.

Lie Number One: "This is the best rate we can offer you." When a loan officer tells you this, what they really mean is, "This is the rate that makes us the most money while still being low enough that you probably won't shop around." Unless you specifically ask to see the par rate, which 99% of borrowers never do, they're going to quote you a marked-up rate. And they'll deliver it with such confidence that you'll never question it.

Lie Number Two: "These fees are standard industry charges." Some fees are legitimate. Appraisal fees, title fees, government recording fees—these are real costs that someone has to pay. But mixed in with those legitimate fees are a bunch of junk charges that exist for no reason other than to pad the lender's profit. Processing fees, underwriting fees, document preparation fees, email delivery fees—I've seen them all, and they're almost entirely profit. But they sound official enough that most people just accept them.

Lie Number Three: "Shopping around won't save you much money." This is perhaps the most damaging lie of all because it keeps people from doing the one thing that would actually protect them: getting multiple quotes. The industry desperately wants you to believe that all lenders are basically the same, that rates are all similar, that it's not worth the hassle to get multiple quotes. This is complete nonsense. I've seen rate spreads of half a percent or more between different lenders for the exact same borrower on the exact same day. On a $300,000 loan, that difference can be worth $30,000 over the life of the mortgage. But if they can convince you not to shop around, they can charge you whatever they want.

What This Means for You

So what do you do with this information? How do you protect yourself from a system that's designed to take advantage of you? That's what the rest of this book is about. I'm going to show you exactly how the extraction happens, who's making money at your expense, and most importantly, how to fight back.

But before we get to the solutions, I need you to understand something critical. This isn't about finding the one honest loan officer who's going to treat you fairly out of the goodness of their heart. This isn't about getting lucky and stumbling into a good deal. This is about arming yourself with enough knowledge that you become unprofitable to rip off.

When you know what your par rate is, when you can identify junk fees, when you understand total cost instead of just monthly payment, when you know what questions to ask and how to demand transparency, you stop being an easy mark. You become a problem customer. The kind of customer that loan officers don't want to deal with because they can't make any money off you. And that's exactly what you want to be.

The retail mortgage industry can't survive an educated consumer base. Their entire business model depends on information asymmetry. Take that away, and the whole thing falls apart. That's what we're going to do in this book. We're going to take away their advantage. We're going to level the playing field. We're going to arm you with the knowledge you need to stop being part of that $847 billion and start keeping your money where it belongs, in your pocket.

Ready to learn how they're doing it? Let's go.

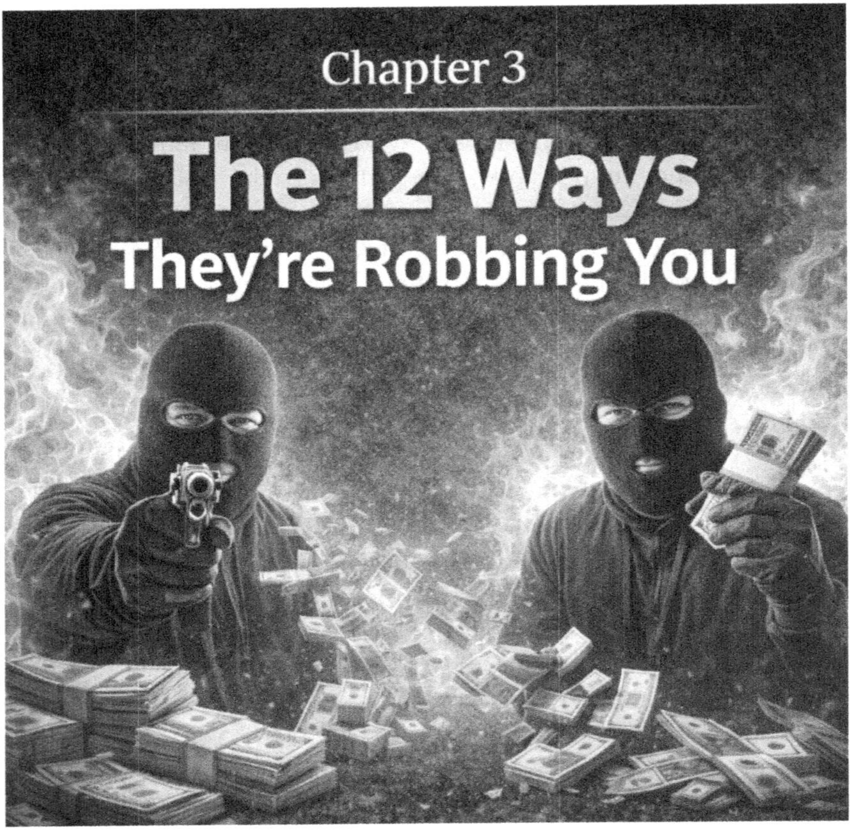

CHAPTER 3

Twelve Ways They're Taking Your Money

I used to keep a list. Not officially. Nothing written down. But in my head, I had this running tally of all the different ways I'd seen loan officers and their companies extract extra money from a single transaction. At first, I thought it was just a few tricks. Maybe four or five different methods. But the longer I stayed in the industry, the longer the list grew. By the time I decided to get out of the retail predatory side of the business, I'd counted twelve distinct extraction methods. Twelve different ways to reach into a borrower's pocket without them noticing.

Here's the thing that'll really get you: most loans don't just use one of these methods. They stack them. I've reviewed loan estimates where the borrower got hit with seven different extraction tactics on the same loan. Seven! Like a prosecutor stacking charges, except instead of a courtroom, it's your kitchen table, and instead of a judge, it's a loan officer with a warm smile and a firm handshake.

As James Clear writes in *Atomic Habits*, "Complexity is the enemy of execution, but it's the best friend of those who profit from confusion. When something is deliberately made too complex to understand, it's usually because someone is making money from your confusion." That's exactly what the mortgage industry has perfected. They've built a system so complex, with so many moving parts, that you can't possibly track where all your money is going.

Let me walk you through all twelve. Pay attention, because odds are you're going to recognize at least three of these from your own mortgage.

Method #1: The Par Rate Concealment From Retail Companies

This is the big one. The foundation that everything else is built on. Every single loan officer in a retail mortgage company has access to something called a rate sheet. It's updated daily, sometimes multiple times a day, and it shows exactly what interest rates you qualify for based on your credit score, amount of downpayment, and loan amount and a bunch of other factors. The rate sheet has dozens of options. But there's one specific rate that matters more than all the others: the par rate.

The par rate is the rate at which the lender makes zero extra money and gives you zero lender credit. It's the baseline. The actual cost. The truth. Let's say you're buying a $375,000 house. Your credit score is 740. Your DTI is 38%. Your down payment is 20%. The rate sheet might show:

- 4.00% = -1.500 points (lender charges you $4,500 points)
- 4.125% = -0.750 points (lender charges you $2,250 points)
- **4.25% = 0.000 points (PAR RATE)**
- 4.375% = +0.625 points (lender gives you $1,875 credit)
- 4.50% = +1.250 points (lender gives you $3,750 credit)
- 4.625% = +1.875 points (lender gives you $5,625 credit)

See that 4.25%? That's what you actually qualify for. That's the real number. But guess what. Your retail lender with "backend warehouse lines" is going to quote you? 4.50%. Maybe 4.625% if they think they can get away with it. Why? Because every eighth percent they mark up above par puts money in the company's pocket. And a chunk of that money ends up in somebody's commission check.

The math: Par rate at 4.25% gives you a monthly payment of $1,475.82. Quoted rate at 4.50% gives you $1,520.06. Difference: $44.24 a month. Doesn't sound like much, right? Here's what that "small" difference actually costs you. Extra per year: $530.88. Extra over 30 years: $15,926.40. Fifteen thousand, nine hundred and twenty-six dollars and forty cents. For nothing. For a rate markup you never knew existed because nobody showed you the par rate.

And that's a conservative markup. I've seen loan officers go a full percentage point above par. That's $65,084.40 over the life of the loan. The red flag: If your loan officer won't show you the rate sheet or explain what par rate means, they're hiding something.

Method #2: The Goldmine for Mortgage Brokers

This is par rate concealment's evil twin. Here's how it works. Retail lenders and banks are not the only ones that can get away with this. Mortgage brokers can sign up for "mini-correspondent" warehouse lines. This means they can create their own rate sheet that is above what the lender actually charges and close the loan. Then they "sell" that loan to the lender for a higher profit. When you take a rate above par, the lender pays the loan officer's company a premium. This is called margin. It's basically a kickback for selling you a more expensive loan than you needed. Let's use that same example. You qualify for 4.25% at par. Your loan officer quotes you 4.50%. That 0.25% markup? The lender pays the mortgage company 1.25 points, which on a $300,000 loan is $3,750. That's instant profit for the company, and a nice commission bump for your loan officer.

Now here's where it gets really insidious. That $3,750 is paid by the lender, not by you directly, so it doesn't show up as a fee on your closing disclosure. It's invisible. You never see it. But you're absolutely paying for it through that higher interest rate over 30 years. The industry loves this because they can tell you with a straight face that they're not charging you anything extra, even though you're about to pay them $15,926 over the life of the loan.

Some states tried to ban yield spread premium (YSP) after the 2008 crisis, but the industry just renamed it and restructured how it's paid. Now it shows up as "lender paid compensation" or gets baked into the rate itself. Different name, same scam. The red flag: If your loan officer talks about "lender paid compensation" but won't show you what rate you'd get without it, they're making money off your rate markup.

Method #3: The "No Closing Cost" Illusion

You've seen the ads. "Refinance with ZERO closing costs!" Sounds amazing, right? Wrong. There's no such thing as a no-cost loan. What they're actually doing is taking a rate significantly above par, using the lender credit that generates to cover your closing costs, and pocketing the difference. Here's a real example from a loan I reviewed. Borrower qualified for 4.25% at par. Closing costs were $4,500. The loan officer quoted them 5.00% and called it a "no closing cost loan." At 5.00%, the lender credit was $7,500. So the lender credit covered the $4,500 in costs and the company pocketed the extra $3,000.

But here's what that "free" loan actually cost the borrower. The difference between 4.25% and 5.00% on a $250,000 loan is $112.20 per month. Over 30 years, that's $40,392. They paid $40,392 to avoid paying $4,500 upfront. And they thought they got a deal. The math literally never makes sense unless you're planning to sell or refinance within 12-18 months. For everyone else, it's a terrible deal disguised as a favor.

The red flag: Any loan officer pushing a "no closing cost" loan without showing you the total cost comparison over time is either incompetent or predatory. Probably both.

Method #4: The Junk Fee Buffet

This one's my personal favorite because of the sheer audacity. Mortgage companies have figured out that they can charge you fees for things that cost them nothing, and most people just pay them without asking questions. I've seen loan estimates with fees like, "processing fee" at $995, "document preparation fee" at $450, "administrative fee" at $695, "email delivery fee" at $125, and my all-time favorite, "file storage fee" at $75.

Let me be clear: these fees cost the lender almost nothing. Processing? That's done by salaried employees as part of their normal job. Document preparation? That's automated software. Email delivery? Are you kidding me? But because they have official-sounding names and they're buried in a long list of legitimate fees like appraisal and title, most people just assume they're required. They're not.

I've seen some lenders charge $2,000 to $3,000 in pure junk fees on a single loan. And when you try to negotiate them away, the loan officer acts like you're asking for something crazy. "Well, these are our standard company fees." Translation: "This is how we extract extra profit from people who don't ask questions."

The red flag: Any fee that sounds like it describes normal business operations, like processing or administration, is probably junk. Ask them to remove it. If they say they can't, ask them to explain exactly what service you're paying for and what it costs the company to provide it. Watch them squirm.

Method #5: The Discount Point Deception

Discount points can be legitimate. You pay money upfront to buy down your interest rate. One point equals 1% of your loan amount, and typically each point lowers your rate by about 0.25%. So on a $300,000 loan, you might pay $3,000 to drop your rate from 4.50% to 4.25%. Sometimes this makes sense, especially if you're planning to stay in the house for a long time.

But here's where the deception comes in. Loan officers will present discount points as if they're always a good deal, without doing the break-even math for you. Using that same example, if you pay $3,000 to save $49 per month, it takes you 61 months, just over five years, to break even. If you sell or refinance before that, you lost money. But most loan officers never explain this. They just say, "For only $3,000, I can get you to 4.25%!" without mentioning that they could have given you 4.25% for free if they'd just shown you the par rate.

Even worse, I've seen loan officers quote people the par rate but make them pay discount points to get it, essentially charging them twice. They mark up from par, then charge you points to get back to where you should have been in the first place. It's brazen.

The red flag: If someone quotes you a rate with discount points without first showing you what rate you qualify for at par, they're either hiding a markup or they're incompetent.

Method #6: The VA Funding Fee Trap

This one specifically targets veterans, which makes it even more disgusting. VA loans require a funding fee, which is a legitimate cost that goes to the VA to fund the program. For most veterans, it's 2.15% of the loan amount on a first-time use, 3.3% on subsequent uses. On a $300,000 loan, that's $6,450 to $9,900. Here's where lenders exploit it. They tell veterans they can roll the funding fee into the loan, which is true. But they don't explain that rolling it in means you're paying interest on that fee for 30 years.

Take that $6,450 funding fee. If you roll it into your loan at 4.50%, you'll pay an additional $5,315.23 in interest on that fee alone over 30 years. That $6,450 fee actually costs you $11,765.23. But nobody explains this to veterans. They just say, "Don't worry, we can roll it in so you don't have to pay anything out of pocket." Technically true. Massively expensive.

Even worse, some loan officers will mark up the rate on VA loans more aggressively because they know veterans trust the VA brand and are less likely to shop around. There is a national name lender that is trusted by veterans because of it's name that exploits veterans with every loan. These men and women trust the company because of their slick marketing, close proximity and "trust" they have built through education. I've seen VA loans with rate markups that would never fly on conventional loans.

The red flag: Any loan officer who doesn't explain the total cost of rolling in the VA funding fee is not looking out for you. Ask them to show you what the fee will actually cost you over the life of the loan, including interest.

Method #7: The Bait-and-Switch Rate Lock

Here's how this scam works. You apply for a loan and the loan officer quotes you a great rate. Let's say 4.25%. You're excited. You tell your friends. You start making plans. Then a week or two later, right before closing, they tell you the rate "changed" and now it's4.50% or 4.625%. They blame it on market conditions, or your credit score, or your debt-to-income ratio, or the appraisal, or underwriting, or literally anything except the truth, which is that they never intended to give you that rate in the first place.

They gave you a teaser rate to get you committed to the process, and now that you're in too deep to back out easily, they hit you with the real rate. This happens because most people don't lock their rate immediately when they apply. They wait until they're further along in the process. And by the time the bait-and-switch happens, you've already paid for the appraisal, you've already scheduled your move, you've already told the seller you're ready to close. The psychological pressure to just accept the new rate and move forward is enormous. There is a national lender that does this with every client to get them sucked into the process and committed and then switches the costs later in the process.

I've watched loan officers do this deliberately. They'll quote an artificially low rate to beat the competition, knowing they'll jack it up later once the borrower is committed.

The red flag: Always ask, "Is this rate locked?" And if it's not, ask them to lock it in writing before you pay a dime. If you don't lock in the interest rate because you are waiting for a potential change in the interest rates, that is fine, but you are definitely gambling with the money. If they won't show you the difference between waiting for a better rate and locking in now, or if they make excuses about why they need to wait, walk away.

Method #8: Appraisal Manipulation

This one's subtle, but it costs borrowers millions. Here's how it works. Let's say you're buying a house for $300,000 with 10% down, so you need a $270,000 loan. The lender orders an appraisal. If the house appraises for exactly $300,000, everything proceeds normally. But if it appraises for $320,000, you've got $20,000 in instant equity. That's great for you, but it's a missed opportunity for the lender.

Some lenders have relationships with appraisers who consistently come in right at the purchase price, never higher. Why? Because if there's extra equity, the borrower might decide to put down less money, which means a bigger loan, which means more interest income for the lender. Or the lender might suggest a cash-out refinance down the road to "access that equity," creating another transaction with more fees.

I'm not saying appraisers are overtly committing fraud. But I am saying that appraisers who consistently deliver values that benefit lenders tend to get more business from those lenders. It's a subtle pressure that shapes behavior over time.

The red flag: If your appraisal comes in exactly at purchase price, that's not necessarily suspicious. But if it happens on multiple properties or if your lender seems unusually cozy with their appraiser, pay attention.

Method #9: Title Company Kickbacks

This is technically illegal under RESPA, but it still happens all the time in creative ways. Here's the basic scam: Your lender refers you to a specific title company. That title company charges you $2,000 for title insurance and services. Of that $2,000, maybe $300 actually goes to pay for the insurance policy. The rest is overhead and profit. The title company then refers business back to the lender, or takes the lender's staff out to fancy dinners, or sponsors the lender's golf tournament, or finds some other creative way to reward the lender for the referral.

You just paid $2,000 for title services that should have cost $1,200, and the extra $800 is essentially funding a kickback scheme. Now, the lender will never call it a kickback. They'll call it a "marketing relationship" or a "marketing services agreement." But the effect is the same. You're overpaying, and your lender is benefiting.

The red flag: If your lender pushes hard for you to use their title company and gets weird when you ask about shopping around, that's a sign. You have the legal right to choose your own title company. Use it.

Method #10: PMI Overcharging

Private Mortgage Insurance is required when you put down less than 20% on a conventional loan. It protects the lender if you default. The cost varies based on your credit score, loan-to-value ratio, and other factors. Here's where the scam comes in. Some lenders will quote you a higher PMI rate than you actually qualify for, pocketing the difference. Or they'll keep PMI on your loan longer than required by law.

By law, PMI must be automatically canceled when your loan balance reaches 78% of the original home value, and you have the right to request cancellation when you hit 80%. But some servicers "forget" to cancel it, hoping you won't notice. I've reviewed loans where borrowers paid PMI for years after they should have hit 78% LTV, simply because nobody told them and they didn't know to ask.

The other trick is lender-paid PMI, where the lender pays your PMI but builds the cost into a higher interest rate. This can sometimes make sense, but often it's more expensive over the long run and it's much harder to get rid of because it's baked into your rate for the life of the loan.

The red flag: Ask explicitly what your PMI rate is, how it's calculated, and at what point it will be removed. Get it in writing. And set a reminder to check your loan balance when you think you're approaching 80% LTV.

Method #11: Escrow Padding

Your lender collects money for property taxes and homeowners insurance in an escrow account, then pays those bills on your behalf. By law, they're allowed to keep a cushion of up to two months of payments in that account to protect against shortages. But some lenders pad the escrow account way beyond what's legally allowed or necessary, effectively using your money as an interest-free loan to themselves.

I've reviewed escrow accounts that were overfunded by $3,000 to $5,000. That's your money, sitting in an account earning nothing for you, while the lender uses it to improve their cash position. And when you eventually pay off the loan or refinance, they're supposed to return that cushion to you, but sometimes it takes months of nagging to actually get your money back.

The red flag: Review your escrow account analysis every year. The servicer is required to send you one. If the cushion is consistently more than two months of payments, demand a refund of the excess.

Method #12: The Servicing Transfer Shell Game

After you close your loan, there's a good chance your lender will sell the servicing rights to another company. This means you'll start making payments to a different servicer than the one who originated your loan. This is legal and common. Here's where it gets shady. In the chaos of the transfer, things get "lost." Your escrow balance doesn't transfer correctly. Your payment due date changes but nobody tells you clearly. Your automatic payment setup gets canceled. Then you get hit with late fees because the new servicer claims they didn't receive your payment on time, even though you paid what you always paid on the date you always paid it.

I've seen borrowers get charged hundreds of dollars in late fees and penalties during servicing transfers, even though they did everything right. The servicers blame each other, nobody takes responsibility, and you're stuck with the fees. Even worse, some servicing transfers are specifically designed to create confusion so they can extract extra fees from borrowers who don't understand what's happening.

The red flag: When you get a notice that your loan is being transferred, immediately contact both the old and new servicer. Verify your exact payoff balance, escrow balance, payment due date, and get confirmation in writing of your first payment to the new servicer. Don't assume anything will transfer smoothly.

The Stack

Here's what makes all of this truly devastating. As Timothy Ferriss points out in *The 4-Hour Workweek*, "The most sophisticated businesses don't rely on one income stream. They stack multiple small extractions that, individually, seem reasonable but collectively represent massive profit. It's death by a thousand cuts, monetized."

That's exactly what happens with mortgages. You don't just get hit with one of these twelve methods. You get hit with five, six, seven at once. They mark up your rate by half a point, charge you $2,500 in junk fees, sell you discount points you don't need, pad your escrow account, and refer you to an overpriced title company. Each extraction seems small enough that you don't fight it. But when you add them all up, you're talking about $40,000, $50,000, $60,000 over the life of your loan.

And the kicker? You'll probably never even realize it happened. You'll make your payment every month, thinking you got a fair deal, completely unaware that you're paying for your loan officer's boat, your lender's quarterly earnings target, and Wall Street's dividend payments.

That is, unless you learn to ask the right questions. Which is exactly what we're about to do.

Part 2
THE VAULT

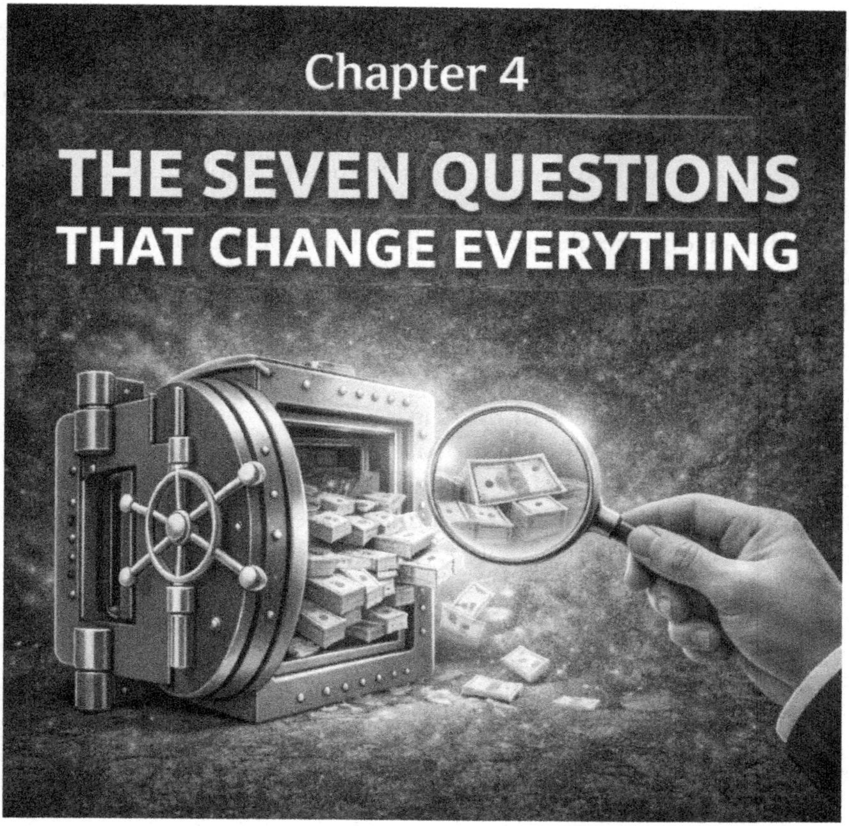

CHAPTER 4

The Seven Questions That Change Everything

Before we dive into the questions, I need to tell you something important. Everything you've read so far, the $847 billion theft, the twelve extraction methods, the profit chain from your loan officer to Wall Street, all of it works because of one thing. You don't know what to ask.

The entire system is built on information asymmetry. They have the rate sheets, you don't. They understand margins and secondary markets, you don't. They know which fees are negotiable, you don't.

That asymmetry is worth billions. But here's the thing about asymmetry: it only takes a few good questions to flip it on its head.

I spent years watching loan officers squirm when a truly informed borrower sat down across from them. Someone who'd done their homework. Someone who knew the industry jargon. Someone who asked the uncomfortable questions that force transparency. Those borrowers got dramatically better deals. Not because they were more likeable or had better credit. Simply because they asked questions that made it expensive to lie.

After reviewing hundreds of these interactions, I noticed a pattern. There were seven specific questions that, when asked correctly, exposed almost everything. Seven questions that force your loan officer to either be honest or reveal themselves as predatory. Seven questions that can save you $30,000 to $60,000 on your mortgage.

As Chris Voss writes in Never Split the Difference, "You can't negotiate from a position of strength if you don't know the baseline. Every negotiation is really about information asymmetry. Whoever has more information has more power. Always establish the true cost before discussing the markup."

Here they are.

Question #1: "What is the par rate I qualify for?"

This is the nuclear option. The par rate question is the single most powerful tool in your arsenal because it forces your loan officer to show you the baseline, the rate at which the lender makes zero extra money. Once you know par, everything else is markup. Every quarter percent above par is profit they're extracting. And once they tell you the par rate, they can't hide behind "competitive rates" or "current market conditions." The number is the number.

I've watched loan officers' faces when borrowers ask about par rate. There's usually a flicker of something, surprise, discomfort, sometimes annoyance. Because this question tells them three things immediately. You've done your homework. You understand how mortgage pricing works. You're not going to accept a marked-up rate without negotiation. In other words, you're not an easy mark.

Most loan officers have never had a single client ask about par rate. Not one. So when you ask it, you're immediately in the top 5% of informed borrowers they've dealt with. And that changes everything.

The dodges you'll hear:

Dodge #1: "We don't really use that terminology anymore." Translation: "I was hoping you didn't know that term existed." Reality: Par rate is still very much a thing. Every rate sheet has a par rate. They just don't want to show it to you. Your response: "Okay, then show me your rate sheet and tell me which rate has zero lender credit. That's par."

Dodge #2: "Every lender calculates it differently, so it's not really a useful comparison." Translation: "I'm going to confuse you with technical nonsense." Reality: Par rate is universal. It's the rate where pricing equals zero. Your response: "I understand different lenders might have different par rates based on their costs, but you still have a par rate for my specific scenario. What is it?"

Dodge #3: "Par rate isn't necessarily your best option. We should focus on the total cost." Translation: "I don't want to show you the baseline because then you'll see my markup." Reality: They're right that par isn't always best, but you still need to see it to make an informed decision. Your response: "I agree, and I want to compare total costs. But I need to see the par rate first so I understand the baseline. Then we can discuss whether paying points to buy down or taking a higher rate makes sense."

The script: Here's exactly what to say. "Before we go any further, I need to know the par rate I qualify for based on my credit, income, and loan amount. I understand you need to make money on this loan, and I respect that. But I need to see the baseline first so I can make an informed decision."

If they refuse after that clear, professional request? Walk away. If they won't show you the baseline price, they're planning to rip you off.

Question #2: "Can I see the actual rate sheet for my scenario?"

If par rate is the foundation, the rate sheet is the master key. Once you're looking at the same document they're looking at, there's nowhere left to hide. The rate sheet shows every rate option you qualify for, the exact pricing at each rate, and what the lender makes at each price point.

Most borrowers have no idea rate sheets even exist. They think their loan officer quotes them a rate based on some mysterious calculation happening in the back office. Wrong. There's a document. A spreadsheet. A pricing engine. And it shows exactly what you qualify for at every rate level.

When you ask to see it, you're asking to pull back the curtain. And most loan officers will resist because the rate sheet exposes the markup immediately.

The dodges you'll hear:

Dodge #1: "That's proprietary information." Translation: "If you see what I see, you'll know I'm overcharging you." Reality: There's nothing proprietary about YOUR pricing options for YOUR loan. Your response: "I understand the rate sheet itself might be your company's document, but I'm asking to see the pricing options for my specific scenario. I'm the customer. I should see what I'm choosing from."

Dodge #2: "It's too complicated and technical. You wouldn't understand it." Translation: "I'm going to condescend to you and hope you back down." Reality: Rate sheets aren't that complicated. Rates go down the left side, pricing goes across the top. Your response: "I appreciate your concern, but I'm comfortable with financial documents. Please show me the rate sheet, and if I have questions, I'll ask."

Dodge #3: "We don't really use rate sheets anymore. It's all done through our pricing engine." Translation: "I'm lying and hoping you don't call my bluff." Reality: Even if it's generated by software, there's still a display showing your pricing options. Your response: "Okay, then show me the screen from your pricing engine that shows all the rate options for my scenario."

What to look for once you have it: First, confirm the par rate. Find the 0.000 pricing point. That's your baseline. Second, see what they're actually proposing. If they quoted you 4.50% and par is 4.25%, you're looking at a 0.25% markup worth about $4,500. Third, look at options below par. Could you take 4.125% and pay $3,000 points or 4.5% and get $4500 toward closing costs? Might make sense if you're short on cash. Fourth, compare across lenders. Get rate sheets from two to three different lenders. Par rates should be similar, within 0.125%. This is the best part of working with a mortgage broker and why I became a mortgage broker. We can shop across over 150 lenders to see who has the rates and fees dialed in the best.

Question #3: "How much are you making on this loan?"

This is the question that makes loan officers shift in their seats. Because here's the uncomfortable truth: in almost every other professional relationship, you know what you're paying. Your lawyer bills you $350 an hour. Your financial advisor charges 1% of assets under management. Your realtor gets 3% of the sale price. But your loan officer? Their compensation is hidden.

Here's what your Loan Estimate shows: Origination Fee at $2,000. Here's what it doesn't show: Margin at $4,500. Their real compensation: $6,500. Your knowledge of their compensation: $2,000. That gap is where they make their money.

By law, lenders are required to disclose loan originator compensation. It's right there in the Dodd-Frank regulations. But here's how they get around it. They disclose the origination fee you're paying directly, but they bury the margin in the rate itself. So technically it's disclosed, because your interest rate is disclosed, but the connection between that rate and their compensation is invisible.

The dodges you'll hear:

Dodge #1: "It's all disclosed on your Loan Estimate." Translation: "It's disclosed in a way that makes it impossible for you to actually understand." Reality: The origination fee is disclosed. The margin isn't, at least not clearly. Your response: "I see the origination fee. I'm asking about your total compensation including any margin or backend compensation from the lender."

Dodge #2: "That's confidential company information." Translation: "I don't want you to know because you'll think it's too much." Reality: It's your money. You have a right to know where it's going. Your response: "I'm not asking about your company's profit margins. I'm asking how much you personally are making from my loan. That's directly relevant to me as the customer."

What's reasonable compensation: For a straightforward purchase or refinance with no complications, fair compensation for a loan officer is 2.75% of the loan amount or less. If it is more than 2.75% of the loan amount, you're being robbed.

Question #4: "Can you show me a break-even analysis for any discount points or lender credits?"

Discount points and lender credits are opposite sides of the same coin. With discount points, you pay money upfront to buy down your interest rate. With lender credits, you take a higher interest rate in exchange for the lender giving you money toward closing costs. Both can be legitimate strategies. But only if the math works in your favor.

The problem is, most loan officers present these options without showing you the break-even calculation. They'll say, "For just $3,000, I can get you to 4.25%!" without telling you it'll take you 62 months to recoup that $3,000 through lower payments. Or they'll say, "We can do a no-closing-cost loan!" without explaining that the higher rate will cost you $42,000 over 30 years to avoid paying $4,500 upfront.

The script: "I'm interested in understanding the break-even point for paying points or taking credits. Can you show me exactly how many months it will take to recoup any upfront costs through lower monthly payments, and what the total cost difference looks like over 5, 10, and 30 years?"

If they can't or won't show you this calculation, it's because the math doesn't work in your favor.

Question #5: "What's the total cost of this loan compared to my other options?"

This is where the monthly payment trap gets exposed. Loan officers love to focus on monthly payment because it sounds small. "Your payment will only go up $87 a month!" Sounds manageable, right? But that $87 a month for 30 years is $31,320. That's the number that matters.

Total cost includes everything: the loan amount, all the interest you'll pay over the life of the loan, all the fees, all the points, everything. When you compare loans, you need to compare total cost, not just monthly payment.

The script: "I need to see a side-by-side comparison showing the total cost of this loan versus my other options, including all fees, all interest, and all payments over the full term. I want to see what I'm paying in total, not just what my monthly payment is."

An honest loan officer will create this comparison for you willingly. A predatory one will resist because total cost comparisons expose exactly how much you're overpaying.

Question #6: "Which of these fees are negotiable?"

There are three categories of fees on your Loan Estimate. First, third-party fees that go to actual service providers like appraisers, title companies, and government recording offices. These are mostly fixed, though you can sometimes shop for better prices. Second, legitimate lender fees for actual services like credit reports and flood certifications. These are usually non-negotiable but should be reasonable. Third, junk fees that exist purely to pad the lender's profit. These are 100% negotiable because they cost the lender nothing.

The problem is, they're all mixed together on your Loan Estimate, and they're designed to look equally legitimate. So you need to ask directly: which fees are negotiable?

The script: "I'm looking at these fees and I'd like to know which ones are negotiable. Specifically, the processing fee, the administration fee, and the document preparation fee. Can you remove or reduce these?"

Watch what happens. An honest loan officer will either remove them without argument, or explain exactly what service each fee pays for. A predatory one will act like you're asking for something crazy and insist that "these are standard company fees."

Fees you should never pay: Email delivery fee, file storage fee, rate lock fee if you're locking at application, courier fees for documents that can be emailed, excessive administrative fees over $200, processing fees over $500, underwriting fees over $1300.

Question #7: "Can you guarantee this rate and these terms in writing before I commit?"

This is your protection against the bait-and-switch. You know the play. They quote you an amazing rate to get you hooked. You start the process, pay for the appraisal, get emotionally invested. Then right before closing, the rate "changes" because of some mysterious market condition or underwriting requirement. Suddenly you're locked in, it's too late to back out easily, and you accept the higher rate because walking away feels impossible.

The only protection against this is to get everything in writing upfront. Before you pay any fees. Before you commit to the process. Before you're in too deep to walk away.

The script: "Before we move forward, I need a written rate lock confirmation that guarantees this specific rate, these specific fees, and these specific terms. I'm not paying any application fees or appraisal fees until I have that guarantee in writing."

If they won't provide it, that tells you everything you need to know. They're planning to change the terms later.

What it should include: The exact interest rate, the exact APR, the lock expiration date, all lender fees itemized, confirmation that the rate won't change unless your financial situation or the property changes, the loan officer's signature and date.

You should also talk with your loan officer if you are planning on “floating” the interest rate if your closing date is further out. Sometimes, this could make sense, but you need the clear picture and upfront knowledge before making this decision.

Using All Seven Questions Together

Here's the power move. You don't ask these questions one at a time over multiple conversations. You ask them all upfront, in your first serious discussion with a loan officer. Here's how that conversation goes.

You: "Before we get too far into this, I have seven questions I need answered. These are deal-breakers for me, so if you're not comfortable answering them clearly, we should probably not waste each other's time."

Then you run through all seven. Par rate. Rate sheet. Compensation. Break-even analysis. Total cost comparison. Negotiable fees. Written guarantee.

One of two things will happen. Either they'll answer everything honestly and you'll know you're dealing with a transparent loan officer, or they'll dodge and deflect and you'll know you need to walk away.

Either way, you win. Because you're either getting transparency or you're saving yourself from getting ripped off.

Tony Robbins puts it perfectly in MONEY Master the Game: "The quality of your life is determined by the quality of the questions you ask. Weak questions get weak answers. Powerful questions force clarity. 'What is the baseline price?' is one of the most powerful questions in any transaction."

These seven questions are your power. Use them.

CHAPTER 5

Breaking the Code: How to Speak the Industry's Secret Language

The mortgage industry doesn't just hide information from you. They hide it in plain sight, wrapped in jargon and technical terminology that sounds official but is designed to confuse. It's like they're speaking a different language, and you're expected to sign a contract worth hundreds of thousands of dollars without understanding half the words on the page.

This isn't an accident. Complexity is profitable. The more confused you are, the less likely you are to ask questions. The less you understand, the easier you are to manipulate. As Malcolm Gladwell writes in Talking to Strangers, "When someone says 'That information is proprietary' in a consumer transaction, what they really mean is 'If you knew what I knew, you wouldn't agree to this deal.' Transparency is the enemy of excessive profit."

So let me translate. I'm going to teach you how to read the two most important documents you'll get during the mortgage process, how to decode the jargon they use to keep you confused, and how to spot the tricks they use to hide what really matters. By the end of this chapter, you'll speak mortgage fluently enough to negotiate like a pro.

Document #1: The Loan Estimate

Within three business days of applying for a mortgage, lenders are required by law to give you a Loan Estimate. It's a standardized three-page form that's supposed to show you all the costs and terms of your loan. It's actually pretty well designed, as far as government forms go. The problem isn't the form itself. The problem is what companies and loan officers do and don't tell you about what's on it.

Let me walk you through it page by page and show you where the bodies are buried.

Page 1: Loan Terms

This is where they show you the big numbers. Loan amount, interest rate, monthly payment. It looks straightforward, but there are tricks hidden even here.

Loan Amount: This should match what you're borrowing. If it's higher than expected, ask why. Sometimes they sneak in the VA funding fee or financed closing costs without explaining it clearly.

Interest Rate: This is the rate you're being quoted. But remember, this isn't necessarily the par rate. This is the rate they want you to take. You need to ask, "What's the par rate I qualify for?" to see if this is marked up.

Monthly Principal & Interest: This is your base payment before taxes and insurance. It's the number they'll focus on because it sounds manageable. Don't fall for it. You need to look at total cost, not just monthly payment.

Estimated Total Monthly Payment: This includes principal, interest, property taxes, homeowners insurance, and mortgage insurance if applicable. This is closer to your real payment, but even this can be misleading if they're estimating your property taxes low. (This happens a lot when lenders try to make things look better than they are)

In 5 Years: Here's a weird one. They show you how much you'll have paid in principal, interest, and total payments after five years. This number is mostly useless for comparison purposes, but it's there because regulations require it. Ignore it and focus on lifetime cost instead.

Annual Percentage Rate (APR): This is supposed to be the "true cost" of your loan because it factors in fees along with interest. In theory, it's useful for comparing loans. In practice, it's misleading because different lenders calculate it differently. Don't rely on APR alone. Ask for total cost instead.

Page 2: Closing Cost Details

This is where the junk fees hide. The form breaks costs into sections, and each section has its own tricks.

Section A: Origination Charges

This is what you're paying the lender directly. It usually includes:

- Origination fee: Often 2% to 2.75% of the loan amount. This is 100% negotiable. If they're charging more than 2.75%, push back hard.

- Application fee: Sometimes they charge $300 to $500 just to apply. This is garbage. Refuse to pay it.
- Administration fee: Another junk fee. Should be included in origination, not charged separately. Negotiate this away.

Section B: Services You Cannot Shop For

This is misleading. The title implies these fees are fixed, but that's not always true. These are services the lender chose, and they often chose them because of referral relationships. Ask if you can use your own providers. Most of the time, they will require these though.

Section C: Services You Can Shop For

Title insurance, settlement fees, survey fees. You absolutely can shop for these. Get quotes from 2-3 providers and choose the cheapest.

Section E: Taxes and Government Fees

These are real and mostly unavoidable. Recording fees, transfer taxes, etc. You can verify these by calling your county recorder's office. If they seem high, double-check.

Section F: Prepaids

Property taxes, insurance, prepaid interest. These are real costs you'd pay anyway, just collected at closing. The only trick here is if they're overestimating your property taxes to make the escrow account bigger.

Section G: Initial Escrow Payment

This is where they collect money for your escrow account to cover future property taxes and insurance. By law, they can collect up to two months of cushion. If they're collecting more, ask why.

Page 3: Comparisons and Additional Information

This page shows you the total you'll pay over the life of the loan. This is actually the most important number on the entire form, but most people skip right past it because it's on page 3 and the numbers are huge. Don't skip it. This is where you see the real cost.

Total of Payments: This is every penny you'll pay over 30 years. Principal, interest, everything. If you're comparing two loans, compare this number.

Finance Charge: Total interest you'll pay over the life of the loan. Again, compare this across lenders.

Document #2: The Closing Disclosure

You'll get this three business days before closing or sooner. It's similar to the Loan Estimate but with final, actual numbers instead of estimates. Your job is to compare the two documents line by line and challenge anything that changed without explanation.

The format is almost identical to the Loan Estimate, which makes comparison easier. But here's what to watch for.

Rate changes: If your interest rate is different from what was on your Loan Estimate, and you had a rate lock, something's wrong. Pull out your rate lock confirmation and demand an explanation.

Fee increases: Small changes are normal. Vendors adjust their exact prices. But if a fee jumped by more than $100, ask why.

New fees: If there's a fee on the Closing Disclosure that wasn't on the Loan Estimate, stop. "What is this $450 courier fee? It wasn't on my Loan Estimate. Why am I being charged this now?"

Lender credit changes: If they promised you a lender credit on the Loan Estimate and it's smaller or gone on the Closing Disclosure, that's a red flag. Get a clear explanation into what happened.

Sometimes, interest rate extensions, a change in down payment amount, low appraisals can change this.

Don't sign until you understand every change. And if something's wrong and they won't fix it, reschedule the closing. Yes, it's awkward. But it's your money.

Decoding the Jargon They Use to Confuse You

Beyond the forms, loan officers use specific terminology designed to make you feel like you don't understand what's happening. Let me translate the most common phrases.

"This is the best rate I can offer you." Translation: "This is the rate that makes me the most money while still being low enough that you probably won't shop around." They're not showing you par rate. They're showing you the marked-up rate they want you to take.

"These fees are standard industry charges." Translation: "These are the fees we charge people who don't ask questions." Nothing is standard. Everything is negotiable except third-party fees that go to actual service providers.

"Your monthly payment will only go up by $87." Translation: "I'm hoping you won't multiply $87 times 360 months and realize that's $31,320." They focus on monthly payment because it sounds small. Always ask for total cost instead.

"We'll give you a no-closing-cost loan." Translation: "We're going to mark up your interest rate significantly and use the extra profit to cover your closing costs. You'll pay way more over time, but you won't notice because we're calling it 'free.'"

"The APR is what really matters for comparison." Translation: "I'm going to use this technical-sounding number that most people don't understand to distract you from asking about total cost."

"Shopping around will hurt your credit score." Translation: "I don't want you talking to my competitors because they might offer you a better deal." Reality: Multiple mortgage inquiries within 45 days count as one inquiry. Shop aggressively.

"You need to lock your rate today or you'll miss this pricing." Translation: "I want your commitment before you have time to get competing quotes." Never lock on the first day unless rates are skyrocketing and you're genuinely about to miss a major rate increase.

"That information is proprietary." Translation: "If I show you the rate sheet, you'll see I'm marking you up." Rate sheets aren't proprietary when it comes to your own pricing options.

"It's too complicated to explain." Translation: "I don't want to explain it because the explanation would reveal I'm overcharging you."

"We don't use that terminology anymore." Translation: "I was hoping you didn't know that term existed, and now I'm going to pretend it's outdated so I don't have to answer your question."

How to Read Between the Lines

Beyond specific phrases, there are patterns in how loan officers communicate that tell you whether they're being honest or hiding something.

Pattern #1: Vague answers to specific questions

You: "What's the par rate I qualify for?" Them: "Well, rates vary depending on a lot of factors, and we'll get you a competitive rate based on your scenario."

That's not an answer. That's a dodge. Press harder.

Pattern #2: Focusing on monthly payment instead of total cost

If they keep steering the conversation back to monthly payment no matter how many times you ask about total cost, they're hiding something.

Pattern #3: Rushing you to commit

"We need to lock this rate today." "I need your application fee now to hold this pricing." "This offer expires at 5 PM."

Artificial urgency is a sales tactic. Legitimate rate locks last 15-60 days. There's rarely a reason to rush. They should be able to show you the difference in rate locks at different lengths of time.

Pattern #4: Getting defensive when you ask questions

Honest loan officers welcome questions. They know that educated clients become long-term referral sources. Predatory loan officers get irritated when you ask questions because questions reveal their tactics.

If someone acts like you're being difficult for asking about par rate or total cost, you're dealing with the wrong person.

The Power of Speaking Their Language

Here's what happens when you learn to decode the industry jargon and speak back to them in their own language.

First, you immediately signal that you're not an easy mark. When you ask about par rate, margins, compensation, total cost comparison, and break-even analysis, the loan officer knows you've done your homework. That changes the entire dynamic.

Second, you can't be confused by technical terminology anymore. When they throw jargon at you, you understand what they're really saying.

Third, you can call out dodges and deflections. When they give you a vague non-answer, you know to press harder.

And fourth, you can negotiate effectively. You can't negotiate from a position of strength if you don't understand what you're negotiating. But once you speak the language, you're dangerous.

Seth Godin writes in Purple Cow, "Remarkable marketing is the art of building things worth noticing right into your product or service. The opposite is making something mediocre and hoping clever advertising will convince people to buy it anyway." The mortgage industry has spent decades on the "mediocre product, clever language" model. They use jargon to make mediocre deals sound remarkable.

But now you know the code. You can see through the language games. You understand what the documents really say. And you know what questions to ask when they try to confuse you.

That makes you unprofitable to rip off. And that's exactly where you want to be.

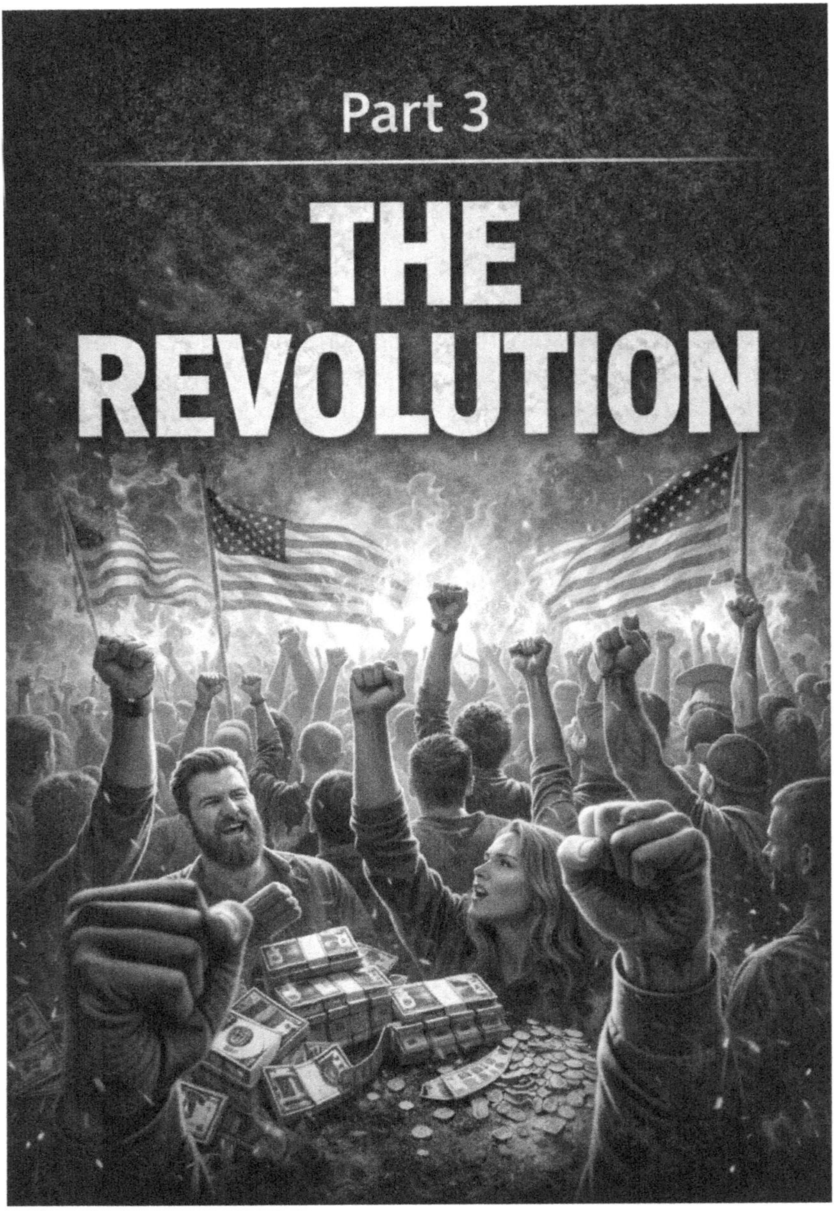
Part 3
THE REVOLUTION

CHAPTER 6

Your Four-Phase Battle Plan

Most people approach getting a mortgage like they're asking for a favor. They find one loan officer, usually a referral from their real estate agent, and hope that person treats them fairly. They answer questions, provide documents, and trust the expert to give them a good deal. That's not a strategy. That's hoping. Hope is not a plan.

As Stephen Covey writes in The 7 Habits of Highly Effective People, "Hope is not a strategy. Wishing is not a plan. If you want different results, you need a different system. Success in any negotiation comes from preparation, not improvisation." Here's what a real plan looks like.

Phase 1: Preparation (Before You Contact Any Lender)

This is where most people skip ahead and cost themselves thousands. They get excited about buying a house and immediately start calling lenders. Big mistake. You need to do your homework first so you're negotiating from strength, not desperation.

Get your real credit scores. Not Credit Karma. Not your credit card's "free score." Your actual FICO scores. Go to myFICO.com and pay $40 for all three scores from Equifax, Experian, and TransUnion. Lenders use the middle score. You need to know what that is before you start shopping. Why pay when free scores exist? Because free scores can be 30 to 50 points different from your FICO score. That difference costs you real money.

What to do with your scores: If all three are within 20 points, use the middle score for planning. If you have big gaps of 50 or more points, pull your credit reports and look for errors. Dispute anything inaccurate. If your score is below 680, you might want to spend two to three months cleaning up credit before applying.

Calculate your real budget. Don't trust online calculators that tell you what you "can afford." They don't know your life. They don't know you're supporting aging parents or saving for IVF or planning to start a business. Here's the real affordability formula: Maximum monthly payment equals your monthly take-home income times 0.28, minus property tax, minus insurance, minus HOA. That 28% is the absolute ceiling. Comfortable is more like 20% to 25%.

If your take-home is $7,000 per month, your maximum payment is $1,960. Minus property tax at $300 leaves $1,660. Minus insurance at $150 leaves $1,510. Your comfortable payment is $1,400 to $1,575. Now you know your real range. Don't let a lender push you higher. Lenders and loan officers calculate based on “before taxes”, not your actual take home pay.

Build your document file. Get everything organized now so you're not scrambling later. You need your last two years of tax returns, last two months of bank statements from all accounts, last two months of pay stubs, W-2s from last two years, photo ID, and proof of any other income like rental or child support. Put it all in one folder. Digital and physical copies.

Research your market. Go to Freddie Mac's Primary Mortgage Market Survey to see national average rates. This gives you a baseline. If someone quotes you 0.5% above the national average, you know they're either marking you up aggressively or you're not as strong a borrower as you thought.

Identify a mortgage broker that can shop at least four to five lenders. Don't put all your eggs in one basket. Mix it up. You can shop one big national lender if you want to see how they are going to rip you off, however, a "true" mortgage broker without any "correspondent/warehouse lines can help make your life a lot easier. This gives you a range of pricing and service models.

Phase 2: Intelligence Gathering (Getting Quotes)

Now you're ready to start contacting a mortgage broker. But you're not applying yet. You're gathering intelligence.

The initial contact script. When you first reach out, here's what you say. "I'm shopping for a mortgage and I'd like to get a preliminary quote before I formally apply. I have my credit score, income, and down payment information ready. Can you give me a rate quote and estimated closing costs based on these numbers?" Notice what you didn't say. You didn't say "I'm ready to apply." You didn't say "My realtor recommended you." You said "I'm shopping." That sets the tone.

Information to provide versus request. Give them your credit score, income, loan amount, down payment, and property location. Don't give them your Social Security number yet. Don't let them pull your credit yet. You're not applying. You're shopping. In return, ask for their best rate quote at par, estimated closing costs broken down by category, and their compensation based on this scenario.

Once the mortgage broker has provided all of this information for several different lenders, you can determine the fees, costs, and rates across the different lenders.

Now narrow to your top two or three based on who had the best pricing and who was most transparent in that initial conversation. This is the easiest way to know if you are working with the right mortgage broker and if it is who you should apply with.

Deep dive with the seven questions. Once you've narrowed it down, have a serious conversation with the loan officer. This is where you ask all seven questions. What is the par rate I qualify for? Can I see the actual rate sheet? How much are you making on this loan? Can you show me a break-even analysis for any discount points or credits? What's the total cost of this loan compared to other options? Which of these fees are negotiable? Can you guarantee this rate and these terms in writing before I commit?

Their answers to these questions will tell you everything you need to know. If they answer clearly and provide documentation, you're dealing with a transparent lender. If they dodge, deflect, or get defensive, walk away.

Phase 3: Negotiation (Getting the Best Deal)

You've got your quotes. You know if they are transparent or not. Now it's time to negotiate.

The leverage play. Take your best offer and use it to negotiate with your mortgage broker. "I really want to work with you because of your service and transparency, can you explain why one quote is 0.25% lower. Can you help me understand?" This works because they know you're serious and you've done your homework. They'll either explain it or show you why the lenders charge different rates.

Fee negotiation line by line. Once you have received a Loan Estimate, go through your Loan Estimate section by section. For every lender fee, ask "Is this negotiable?" For origination fees, processing fees, underwriting fees, administrative fees, ask them if there is a way to reduce or remove them.

Lock timing strategy. Don't lock your rate on day one unless rates are genuinely skyrocketing. Here's the smart play. Get approved and clear any conditions first. Watch rates daily, your loan officer should help with this. Lock when rates dip or when you're 30 to 45 days from closing. Get written confirmation immediately. If rates drop after you lock, ask about a float-down option. Some lenders offer this for a fee, usually $500 to $1,000. If rates drop significantly, it might be worth it.

Phase 4: Protection (Closing Without Getting Screwed)

You're locked. You're approved. You're two to three weeks from closing. This is when they try to slip in last-minute changes. Stay vigilant.

Document review checklist. You'll get a Closing Disclosure three business days before closing. This is the final numbers. Compare it to your Loan Estimate line by line. Interest rate should match. Loan amount should match. Origination fee should match. Look for small differences under $50, which are normal as vendors adjust their exact fees. Big differences over $100 require explanation.

If something changed significantly, speak up. "My Loan Estimate shows $1,200 for title insurance. The Closing Disclosure shows $1,600. What changed and why wasn't I notified earlier?" Don't close until you get a satisfactory answer.

Last-minute rate change defense. If your rate changed between the Loan Estimate and Closing Disclosure, pull out your rate lock confirmation. "According to my rate lock dated [DATE], my rate is guaranteed at 4.375% until [EXPIRATION DATE]. Nothing material changed in my application. This needs to be corrected before I sign." They'll either fix it immediately because it was an error, explain what changed in your application that triggered repricing, or refuse to honor the lock. If they refuse, don't sign. Escalate to their manager. File complaints. Walk if necessary.

Closing table power move. At the actual closing, you're sitting with a title agent and a stack of documents. The title agent is not your advocate. They work for the title company. Their job is to get you to sign, not to explain every detail. Before you sign anything, say this. "I'd like five minutes to review the final figures on the Closing Disclosure one more time." Take your time. Compare it to the Loan Estimate you reviewed earlier. If anything looks different and wasn't explained in advance, stop. "I see a $450 courier fee that wasn't on my previous Closing Disclosure. What is this for?"

Don't let anyone rush you. This is hundreds of thousands of dollars. You get to take your time. If something's wrong and they won't fix it, don't sign. "I'm not comfortable signing this today. I need to review these changes with my loan officer. We'll need to reschedule." Yes, it's awkward. Yes, the seller might be annoyed. Yes, the title company will be frustrated. But you know what's more frustrating? Paying an extra $450 or $4,500 because you were too polite to push back.

Post-closing check. After you close, you're not done. Within seven days, verify your first payment amount matches what was disclosed, check that your escrow account has the right balance, and confirm your loan was sold or wasn't as they told you. Save all documents in a secure place. Within 30 days, check your credit report to make sure the new loan is reporting correctly, set up autopay for your mortgage so you don't miss that first payment, and review your homeowner's insurance because sometimes lenders require more coverage than necessary.

Within 90 days, if anything feels off, payment amount is wrong, escrow is messed up, customer service is terrible, file complaints with your lender's customer service, CFPB at consumerfinance.gov/complaint, your state's banking regulator, and the Better Business Bureau. Don't wait. Document problems early.

As Adam Grant writes in Think Again, "Amateurs wing it. Professionals follow a system. The difference between getting a good deal and getting ripped off usually comes down to whether you had a plan before you walked into the negotiation."

This four-phase battle plan is your system. Follow it and you'll save tens of thousands of dollars. Skip steps and you'll end up like everyone else, wondering where all your money went.

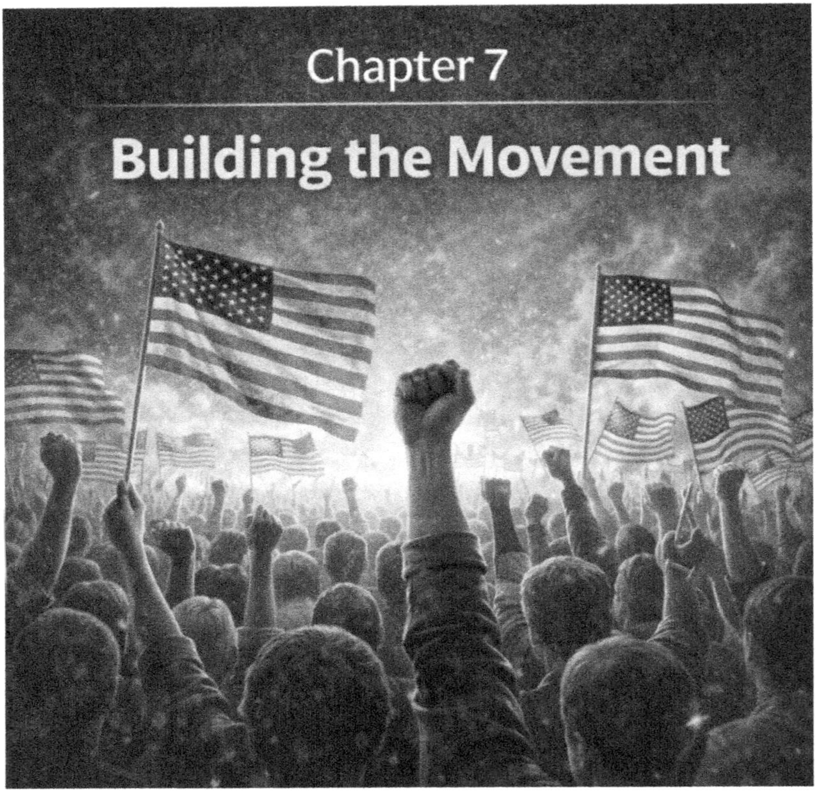

CHAPTER 7

Building the Movement: Why One Informed Borrower Can't Change the System, But a Million Can

When I started being transparent with my clients, showing them rate sheets and explaining exactly what I was making, something interesting happened. I provided what my team calls a "Green Sheet". Why is it called that? Because it is "GREEN". But it shows everything we talked about here in this book. It is a clear and transparent way to show all of the costs in a format that allows you to pick your own interest rate.

Some of my colleagues laughed at me. "You're leaving money on the table, Michael." Others got angry. "You're making the rest of us look bad." A few just shook their heads and said, "You've got twelve kids. You can't afford to run your business like that."

But here's what they didn't see coming. Once I became a mortgage broker with transparent pricing and a transparent mindset, within six months, my referral business exploded. Clients who'd never sent a single referral in their lives were suddenly telling everyone they knew about me. Not because I was the nicest guy or had the best marketing, but because I'd shown them something they'd never seen before in the mortgage industry. Transparency.

And then something even more interesting started happening. Other loan officers started reaching out to me. Quietly at first. "Hey Michael, I saw what you're doing. I've been wanting to operate that way but didn't think it was possible to make a living. How are you doing it?"

That's when I realized something important. I'm not alone. There are loan officers all over this country who are tired of the retail model, the "rip off" model, the predatory model, who want to build businesses on integrity instead of extraction, who are looking for a better way.

That's when the KEEP THE CASH movement was born.

What KEEP THE CASH Actually Is

KEEP THE CASH isn't a company. It's not a franchise. It's not a licensing program. It's a network of like-minded mortgage professionals across the country who have committed to radical transparency. We're brokers and loan officers who've decided that we'd rather make a fair living helping people than make a fortune ripping them off.

Here's how it works. Every member of the KEEP THE CASH network signs a transparency pledge. We commit to showing every client the par rate. We commit to full disclosure of our compensation. We commit to explaining every fee. We commit to comparing total costs, not just monthly payments. And we commit to putting everything in writing before asking for any commitment.

If a KEEP THE CASH loan officer violates these principles, they're out. No second chances. No excuses. Because trust is everything, and one bad actor can destroy what we're building.

Right now, we've got loan officers in 49 states. They are independent mortgage brokers like me. What unites us isn't our business model. It's our commitment to putting borrowers first.

When you work with a KEEP THE CASH loan officer, you're not hoping for transparency. You're guaranteed it. Because we've all staked our reputations on operating differently than the rest of the industry.

Why This Can't Just Be About Me

I need to be honest with you about something. I can't fix the mortgage industry by myself. I'm one loan officer in Tennessee. I close maybe 75-100 loans a year. That's great for my clients, but it's a rounding error in an industry that originates 7 million mortgages annually.

Even if I spent the rest of my career being radically transparent with every single one of my clients, I'd maybe save a few thousand people from getting ripped off. That's meaningful for those families, but it doesn't change the system. The other 6,998,500 mortgages? They're still getting the same predatory treatment.

That's why this has to be bigger than me. As Malcolm Gladwell writes in The Tipping Point, "Change doesn't come from the top down—it comes from the bottom up. When enough consumers refuse to accept predatory practices, industries are forced to change. Your individual action, multiplied across millions of people, becomes a movement."

The mortgage industry will only change when it becomes unprofitable to operate the old way. And that happens in two ways. First, through educated borrowers who refuse to accept predatory pricing. That's you. Second, through honest loan officers who prove you can build a successful business on transparency. That's the KEEP THE CASH network.

The Consumer Revolution

Here's what I'm building, and I want you to be part of it. A network of informed borrowers who refuse to be stolen from. People who ask the hard questions. People who demand transparency. People who walk away from predatory lenders. When enough people do this, the industry has to change.

Right now, they can get away with overcharging because 95% of borrowers don't know any better. Most people walk into the mortgage process thinking all lenders are basically the same, that rates are rates and fees are fees, and that shopping around maybe saves you a couple hundred bucks at most. They don't realize they're about to lose $40,000 or $50,000 over the life of the loan.

But what happens when it's 50%? When half of all borrowers demand to see the par rate, negotiate fees, and compare total costs? When half of all borrowers refuse to work with loan officers who won't show them the rate sheet? Predatory pricing stops being profitable. Transparency becomes the competitive advantage. The loan officers who've been building businesses on deception start losing deals to the ones who've been honest all along.

That's the revolution. Not a regulatory change, though that would help. Not a lawsuit, though those happen. Not a government intervention, though we need that too. A consumer revolution. Millions of educated borrowers voting with their feet and their wallets.

You're part of that. Every time you ask the seven questions, you're making it harder for the industry to steal. Every time you walk away from a bad deal, you're sending a message: "We're not falling for this anymore." Every time you share this knowledge with someone else, you're expanding the movement.

Finding a KEEP THE CASH Loan Officer

If you want to work with someone in the KEEP THE CASH network, here's how to find them. Go to KeepTheCash.com and click on "Find a Loan Officer." You'll see a map of the United States. Click on your state and you can fill out a contact form to have a loan officer reach out to you and get you connected with a KEEP THE CASH loan officer.

Now, I need to be clear about something. KEEP THE CASH loan officers aren't necessarily going to have the absolute lowest rates in your market. We're not a discount service. We're professionals who deserve fair compensation for our expertise. What we guarantee is transparency about that compensation. You'll know exactly what we're making, and you'll be able to compare it against other options to make an informed decision.

Sometimes our rates will be the best. Sometimes they won't be. But you'll always know exactly where you stand, and you'll never wonder if you're being ripped off.

If you have any questions or concerns or need 2nd opinion on your specific scenario, send me an email at michael@keepthecash.com and tell me about your experience.

For Loan Officers Reading This

If you're a loan officer or mortgage broker reading this book, and you're tired of the way the industry operates, I want to talk to you. Maybe you've been feeling the same tension I felt. Making good money but feeling guilty about how you're making it. Closing loans but losing sleep over whether you're really helping people or just extracting from them.

You don't have to keep operating that way. There's a better model. You can build a thriving business on transparency and referrals instead of manipulation and volume. It's possible. I'm doing it. Many others in the KEEP THE CASH network are doing it. And we want to help you do it too.

Go to KeepTheCash.com and click "For Loan Officers." Read about our transparency pledge. And if you're ready to make the change, apply to join. We vet every applicant carefully because this only works if everyone in the network actually walks the talk. But if you're serious about changing how you do business, we want you with us.

The Realistic Expectation

I need to be honest with you about something. Not every loan officer is going to give you perfect answers to all seven questions, even outside the predatory majority. Some will be defensive. Some will dodge. Some will tell you they can't provide certain information. That's okay. The questions aren't just about getting information. They're about revealing character.

A loan officer who gets defensive when you ask about their compensation? Red flag. Walk away. A loan officer who says "Let me check on that and get back to you"? Green flag. They're being honest about not knowing something. A loan officer who willingly shows you the rate sheet and explains everything? Unicorn. Lock them in.

You're not just gathering data. You're filtering for integrity. The loan officers who answer these questions honestly are the ones worth working with, even if their rates aren't the absolute lowest. Because transparency has value. Working with someone you trust has value. Knowing you're getting a fair deal has value. Sometimes that's worth an extra $500 or $1,000 in total cost. But it's never worth $30,000 or $40,000. Know the difference.

The Long Game

As Robert Kiyosaki writes in Rich Dad Poor Dad, "Knowledge without action is just entertainment. The difference between knowing what to do and actually doing it is the difference between poverty and prosperity. Make your commitment tangible by putting it in writing."

Here's my long game, and I'm inviting you to be part of it. I want KEEP THE CASH loan officers in all 50 states. I want us to collectively close 50,000 loans a year with full transparency. That's less than 1% of the total market, but it's enough to start shifting industry norms. Within ten years, I want transparency to be the expectation, not the exception. I want borrowers to be shocked when a loan officer won't show them the rate sheet, instead of being shocked when one does.

This won't happen through regulation. It won't happen through lawsuits. It will happen because enough borrowers demand it and enough loan officers deliver it. It will happen because the economics shift and transparency becomes more profitable than deception. It will happen because we build it, one loan at a time, one referral at a time, one converted loan officer at a time.

You're part of that. Every time you use what you've learned in this book, you're building the movement. Every time you refer someone to a KEEP THE CASH loan officer, you're building the movement. Every time you share this information with a friend or family member who's about to buy a house, you're building the movement.

The vault is unlocked. The truth is in your hands. The movement is growing. Now go use it, share it, and help us change an industry that's been stealing from American families for far too long.

Keep your cash. And help others keep theirs.

APPENDICES
INDUSTRY SECRETS
RED FLAG CHECKLIST
EMAIL TEMPLATES
STATE BY STATE MORTAGE RESOURCES

APPENDIX A: THE 7 QUESTIONS THAT EXPOSE EVERYTHING

Print this card. Laminate it. Keep it with you during every mortgage conversation.

QUESTION 1: "What is the par rate I qualify for?"
Forces disclosure of the baseline rate with zero markup. Any resistance to this question is a red flag.

QUESTION 2: "Can I see the actual rate sheet for my scenario?"
Reveals all pricing options, not just the ones they want to show you. Transparency starts here.

QUESTION 3: "How much are you making on this loan?"
Exposes total compensation including any hidden fees. Fair compensation is 2%-2.75% or less.

QUESTION 4: "Can you show me a break-even analysis for any discount points or credits?"
Prevents you from paying upfront costs you'll never recoup. Demand the math in writing.

QUESTION 5: "What's the total cost of this loan compared to other options?"
Stops the monthly payment trap. Focus on lifetime cost, not just monthly numbers.

QUESTION 6: "Which of these fees are negotiable?"
Identifies junk fees and gives you leverage. Almost everything lender-controlled is negotiable.

QUESTION 7: "Can you guarantee this rate and these terms in writing before I commit?"
Protects against bait-and-switch. No written guarantee = no commitment from you.

IF THEY WON'T ANSWER THESE QUESTIONS CLEARLY, WALK AWAY.

APPENDIX B: THE TEMPLATES

Understanding YOUR personality type helps you communicate more effectively with loan officers. These templates are designed to help you ask the seven questions in a way that feels natural and comfortable for YOUR communication style while still getting the information you need.

Pick the templates that match YOUR personality type:

D (Dominance) - The Direct Communicator: You value efficiency and results. You don't waste time. You ask direct questions and expect direct answers.

I (Influence) - The Relationship Builder: You value connection and positive interactions. You want to like the people you work with. You prefer friendly, collaborative conversations.

S (Steadiness) - The Thoughtful Inquirer: You value harmony and careful decision-making. You don't like conflict. You prefer calm, considerate approaches to big decisions.

C (Conscientiousness) - The Analytical Researcher: You value accuracy and data. You want all the facts. You prefer detailed, systematic analysis before decisions.

QUESTION 1 TEMPLATES: "What is the par rate I qualify for?"

D (Direct) Version:

Subject: Par Rate Required

[Name],

I need the par rate for my scenario:
Credit: [XXX], Loan: $[XXX], Down: [XX]%, Property: [City, State]

Send me: (1) Par rate, (2) Your proposed rate, (3) 30-year cost difference

Comparing lenders this week. Fast response with transparency wins.

[Your Name]

I (Relationship) Version:

Subject: Quick Rate Question - Excited to Work Together!

Hi [Name]!

I really enjoyed our conversation! Before I decide, I want to make sure I understand everything.

I've learned that knowing the "par rate" helps me see the full picture. Could you help with that?

My scenario: Credit [XXX], Loan $[XXX], Down [XX]%, Property: [City, State]

I'd love to see: Par rate, your recommended rate, and how they compare!

I'm talking with a few lenders (want to make the best choice!), and I really appreciate your help!

Thanks!
[Your Name]

S (Thoughtful) Version:

Subject: Par Rate Information Request

Hello [Name],

Thank you for your help with my mortgage. I appreciate your patience as I work through this decision.

I've been researching and learned it's important to understand the "par rate." I hope you don't mind me asking for this.

My details: Credit [XXX], Loan $[XXX], Down [XX]%, Property: [City, State]

Could you provide: Par rate, your proposed rate, and the difference?

I know this might be unusual, but it would help me feel confident. I want to work with someone I can trust.

Thank you,
[Your Name]

C (Analytical) Version:

Subject: Request for Par Rate Documentation

[Name],

I require specific data for my mortgage comparison analysis.

Borrower Profile:
FICO: [XXX], Loan: $[XXX,XXX], LTV: [XX.XX]%
Property: [Type], Occupancy: [Primary/Second/Investment]
Location: [City, State, ZIP]

Required Data:
1. Par rate (0.000 pricing point)
2. Proposed rate
3. Pricing adjustment (basis points + dollar amount)
4. Total interest differential over 360 months

Timeline: 24-48 hours
Format: Email or PDF documentation

Regards,
[Your Name]

QUESTION 2 TEMPLATES: "Can I see the actual rate sheet?"

D (Direct) Version:

Subject: Need Rate Sheet

[Name],

Send me your rate sheet for my scenario. I want to see all options, not just your recommendation.

My scenario: [Credit/Loan Amount/LTV details]

Need: Complete rate sheet (screenshot or PDF) showing all pricing tiers.

Deciding this week. Full transparency gets the deal.

[Your Name]

I (Relationship) Version:

Subject: Let's Look at All the Options Together!

Hi [Name]!

I think it would be really helpful if we could look at the rate sheet together! I've heard this helps borrowers feel more confident.

Could you share the rate sheet for my scenario? I'd love to go through it with you and understand the different choices!

I think it'll make our working relationship even stronger. Can't wait to see what we're working with!

[Your Name]

S (Thoughtful) Version:

Subject: Rate Sheet Review Request

Hello [Name],

I hope you're doing well. I've been thinking about our conversation, and I'd feel more comfortable if I could review the rate sheet.

I know this might be unusual, but it would really help me feel secure about this big decision. Would you be willing to share it?

I'm not trying to make things difficult - I just want to make sure I understand all my options for my family's future.

Thank you for your patience,
[Your Name]

C (Analytical) Version:

Subject: Request for Complete Rate Sheet Documentation

[Name],

To conduct thorough analysis, I require the complete rate sheet for my profile.

Borrower Specs:
FICO: [XXX/XXX/XXX], Loan: $[XXX], LTV: [XX.XX]%
DTI: [XX.XX]%, Property: [Type], Occupancy: [Status]

Required Documentation:
1. Current rate sheet for exact scenario
2. All rate/pricing combinations
3. Adjustment factors (property type, occupancy, loan amount)
4. Lock period options and costs

Purpose: Comparative analysis across lenders using total cost calculations

Delivery: 24 hours

Respectfully,
[Your Name]

QUESTION 3 TEMPLATES: "How much are you making on this loan?"

D (Direct) Version:

Subject: Compensation Disclosure Required

[Name],

Before I commit, I need your total compensation breakdown:
1. Origination fee (what I pay)
2. lender-paid comp
3. Total dollars you're making

Standard is 2%-2.75%. Over $15,000 needs justification.

I respect that you earn money. I don't respect hiding how much.

[Your Name]

I (Relationship) Version:

Subject: Transparency Question - Building Trust!

Hey [Name]!

I know we're building a great relationship, and transparency is so important for trust!

Could you help me understand your total compensation? I'm looking for:
What I'm paying directly (origination fee)
What the lender pays you
Your total earnings

I've read $2,500-$4,000 is standard, and I totally respect you deserve fair pay! I just want us on the same page.

Thanks for being open!

[Your Name]

S (Thoughtful) Version:

Subject: Compensation Question - Hope This Is Okay

Hi [Name],

I hope you don't mind me asking, but I've been advised to understand the compensation structure.

I don't want to offend you, but could you share:
Origination fee I'm paying
Additional compensation from lender
Your total compensation

I've learned 2%-2.75% is typical, which seems fair. I just want to understand clearly.

Thank you for understanding,
[Your Name]

C (Analytical) Version:

Subject: Request for Complete Compensation Breakdown

[Name],

Pursuant to TILA-RESPA regulations, I request complete loan originator compensation documentation.

Required Breakdown:
1. Borrower-paid: Origination $[XXX], Processing $[XXX], Other $[XXX], Subtotal $[XXX]

2. Lender-paid: Compensation (basis points [XXX]), Dollar equivalent $[XXX], Pricing from par [X.XXX]%
3. Total compensation: $[XXX]
4. Percentage of loan: [X.XX]%

Benchmark: 2%-2.75% standard. Over $15,000 requires justification with service breakdown.

Response: 48 hours with rate sheet showing par vs. locked rate.

Regards,
[Your Name]

QUESTION 4 TEMPLATES: "Show me break-even analysis for points/credits"

D (Direct) Version:

Subject: Need Break-Even Math

[Name],

You're proposing $[X],000 in points to get [X.XX]%.

Send me:
1. Monthly savings vs. not paying points
2. Break-even in months
3. 5-year and 10-year total cost comparison

Need the math before deciding. Quick spreadsheet works.

[Your Name]

I (Relationship) Version:

Subject: Help Me Understand the Points Decision!

Hi [Name]!

I want to make a smart decision about points! Could you create a simple breakdown?

Monthly savings by paying points
How long to break even
Total cost at 5, 10, and 30 years

Seeing it laid out will help me feel confident! You're so good at explaining things!

Thanks!
[Your Name]

S (Thoughtful) Version:

Subject: Request for Break-Even Analysis

Hello [Name],

I've been thinking about discount points, and I'd feel more comfortable with a detailed breakdown.

Would you mind showing:
Monthly payment with/without points
Months to break even
Total cost at different periods (5, 10, 30 years)

Having this will help me make the right choice and sleep better knowing I decided well.

Thank you,
[Your Name]

C (Analytical) Version:

Subject: Comprehensive Break-Even Analysis Required

[Name],

I require detailed break-even analysis for discount points/lender credit options.

Scenario Parameters:
Base: $[XXX,XXX]
Option A: [X.XXX]% with $[X],XXX points
Option B: [X.XXX]% at par
Option C: [X.XXX]% with $[X],XXX credit

Required Calculations (Excel preferred):
1. Monthly P&I for each option
2. Cumulative cost at: 12, 36, 60, 84, 120, 360 months
3. Break-even month calculation
4. Net savings/(loss) at 84 months
5. Stated assumptions

Format: Excel with visible formulas
Timeline: 24 hours

Regards,
[Your Name]

QUESTION 5 TEMPLATES: "What's total cost vs. other options?"

D (Direct) Version:

Subject: Total Cost Comparison Needed

[Name],

Give me total cost for all options:
30-year fixed at [X.XX]%
15-year fixed at [X.XX]%
[Other options]

For each: Total payments, total interest, total fees.

Bottom line numbers drive my decision.

[Your Name]

I (Relationship) Version:

Subject: Let's Compare All Our Options!

Hey [Name]!

Before we lock in, I'd love to see options side by side!

Could you create an easy comparison showing:
Different terms (30-year, 15-year, etc.)
Total I'd pay over life of each loan
Interest vs. principal breakdown

Seeing it together will make me super confident!

Thanks a million!
[Your Name]

S (Thoughtful) Version:

Subject: Help Me Compare Total Costs

Hi [Name],

I hope I'm not being too much trouble, but I'd like to see total cost comparisons.

Monthly payment matters, but I want to think about long-term impact on my family.

Could you show:
Total over full term for each option
How much is interest
Savings/extra cost with different choices

I value your patience with my questions.

Thank you,
[Your Name]

C (Analytical) Version:

Subject: Comprehensive Total Cost Analysis Required

[Name],

I require total cost of ownership comparison across all loan structures.

Scenarios:
1. 30-year fixed: [X.XXX]%, $[XXX] fees
2. 15-year fixed: [X.XXX]%, $[XXX] fees
3. [Additional scenarios]

For Each:
Upfront: Closing costs, cash required, prepaids, escrow
Monthly: P&I, taxes, insurance, PMI, HOA, total

Lifetime: Total payments, principal, interest, fees, grand total
Comparison: Monthly difference, total difference, effective APR

Format: Excel with formulas
Delivery: 48 hours

Regards,
[Your Name]

QUESTION 6 TEMPLATES: "Which fees are negotiable?"

D (Direct) Version:

Subject: Fee Negotiation Required

[Name],

Challenging these fees on your Loan Estimate:
Origination: $[X],XXX (reduce to $1,500)
Processing: $XXX (remove)
Underwriting: $XXX (remove)
Admin: $XXX (remove)

Other quotes don't have these. Match or beat them.

Best and final within 24 hours.

[Your Name]

I (Relationship) Version:

Subject: Quick Fee Question - Let's Work Together!

Hi [Name]!

I've been comparing estimates and noticed some fee differences. I know you want to give me the best deal!

I'm seeing: Processing $XXX, Underwriting $XXX, Admin $XXX

Other lenders aren't charging some of these. Can we work together to make your offer more competitive? I really like working with you!

Thanks for being awesome!
[Your Name]

S (Thoughtful) Version:

Subject: Question About Fees

Hello [Name],

I hope this doesn't seem confrontational, but I wanted to ask about some fees.

Processing $XXX, Underwriting $XXX, Administrative $XXX

Other lenders aren't charging all of these. Is there flexibility? I enjoy working with you and would prefer to stay if we can make it work.

Thank you for understanding,
[Your Name]

C (Analytical) Version:

Subject: Fee Justification and Negotiation

[Name],

Upon review of Loan Estimate [date], I identified fees requiring clarification.

Section A Fees:
A.01 Origination $[X],XXX: Request itemized services. Market: $1,500-$2,000. Action: Reduce
A.02 Processing $XXX: What services beyond origination? Market: Included. Action: Remove/justify
A.03 Underwriting $XXX: In-house/outsourced? Cost basis? Market: $300-500. Action: Reduce
A.04 Admin $XXX: What tasks? Market: Junk fee. Action: Remove

Supporting Docs: Attached competing estimates

Request: Justification OR revised estimate at market rates

Timeline: 48 hours

Regards,
[Your Name]

QUESTION 7 TEMPLATES: "Guarantee rate and terms in writing"

D (Direct) Version:

Subject: Written Rate Lock Required Now

[Name],

Before moving forward, send written rate lock:
Rate: [X.XXX]%

Lock: [XX] days
Fees locked (no increases)
Your signature

Email in 2 hours or I lock elsewhere.

[Your Name]

I (Relationship) Version:

Subject: Let's Lock This In - Exciting!

Hey [Name]!

So excited to move forward! Before the next step, let's get rate and terms locked in writing so we're both protected!

Could you send confirmation with: exact rate, lock period, agreed fees, your signature?

This will make us both feel great about moving forward!

Can't wait!
[Your Name]

S (Thoughtful) Version:

Subject: Written Rate Lock Request

Hi [Name],

Thank you for all your help. Before we proceed, I need everything in writing to feel secure.

Could you send written confirmation with: interest rate, lock duration, locked fees, your signature?

I know this is standard, and it will help me feel comfortable moving forward.

Thank you,
[Your Name]

C (Analytical) Version:

Subject: Formal Rate Lock Agreement Required

[Name],

Prior to fees/credit authorization, I require formal written rate lock with:

Rate Specs: Rate [X.XXX]%, APR [X.XXX]%, Type [Fixed/ARM], Lock [XX] days, Expiration [MM/DD/YYYY]

Fee Lock: Itemized lender fees with "will not increase" statement, Total $[X],XXX

Conditions: Void circumstances (specific, limited to material changes), Float-down terms, Extension fees

Legal Statement: "Rate guaranteed by [Lender], unchangeable except conditions listed"

Signatures: Your signature, NMLS, date, company seal

Format: PDF
Timeline: Before any payment/credit pull

Regards,
[Your Name]

APPENDIX C: RED FLAG CHECKLIST

The mortgage industry has developed coded language to hide predatory practices. When you hear these phrases, you're likely being set up for overcharging. Here's how to decode what they're really saying.

RED FLAG CATEGORY 1: Rate and Pricing Deflections

What They Say: "This is the best rate I can offer you."
What It Really Means: "This is the rate that makes me the most money while still being low enough that you probably won't shop around."
Your Response: "What is the par rate I qualify for? I need to see the baseline before I can evaluate your offer."

What They Say: "We don't really use par rate terminology anymore."
What It Really Means: "I was hoping you didn't know that term existed and I could hide the markup."
Your Response: "Every lender has a rate where pricing equals zero. Show me your rate sheet and point to that rate."

What They Say: "Every lender calculates it differently, so par rate isn't a useful comparison."
What It Really Means: "I'm trying to confuse you with technical nonsense so you'll stop asking."
Your Response: "I understand that different lenders may have different par rates based on their costs. What is YOUR company's par rate for my specific scenario?"

What They Say: "Par rate isn't necessarily your best option."
What It Really Means: "I don't want to show you the baseline because then you'll see my markup."
Your Response: "I agree it might not be my best option, but I still need to see it to make an informed decision. Show me par, show me the options above and below it, and then we can discuss which makes sense."

What They Say: "Rates change every day, so I can't guarantee any specific number until you're ready to lock."
What It Really Means: "I'm going to quote you a teaser rate now and jack it up later when you're too committed to walk away."
Your Response: "I understand rates fluctuate. Give me today's rate and lock it in writing. If I decide to wait, we can re-lock at whatever rate is current at that time. But if we're moving forward, lock it now with written confirmation."

What They Say: "I can get you an amazing rate, but you need to lock today or you'll miss it."
What It Really Means: "I don't want you talking to competitors because they might offer better pricing."
Your Response: "If the rate is that good, it will still be good tomorrow after I get competing quotes. If it's not good tomorrow, then it wasn't really that good today."

RED FLAG CATEGORY 2: Fee and Cost Deflections

What They Say: "These fees are standard industry charges."
What It Really Means: "These are the fees we charge people who don't ask questions."
Your Response: "Which specific fees are you referring to as 'standard'? I need to know which ones are for actual third-party services and which ones are your company's fees. And of your company's fees, which are negotiable?"

What They Say: "That information is proprietary."
What It Really Means: "If I show you the rate sheet, you'll see exactly how much I'm marking you up."
Your Response: "The rate sheet showing MY pricing options for MY loan is not proprietary to me as the customer. Either show it to me, or I'll work with a lender who will."

What They Say: "It's all disclosed on your Loan Estimate."
What It Really Means: "It's disclosed in a way that makes it impossible for you to actually understand what you're paying."
Your Response: "I see the origination fee on the Loan Estimate. I'm asking about your TOTAL compensation or backend compensation from the lender. What is the total dollar amount you're making from my loan?"

What They Say: "Your monthly payment will only go up by $87."
What It Really Means: "I'm hoping you won't multiply $87 times 360 months and realize that's $31,320."
Your Response: "What is the total cost over the life of the loan? I need to see total interest paid, total fees paid, and total of all payments for each option."

What They Say: "We'll give you a no-closing-cost loan."
What It Really Means: "We're going to mark up your interest rate significantly and use that profit to cover your closing costs. You'll pay WAY more over time."
Your Response: "Show me the total cost of a no-closing-cost loan versus paying the costs upfront at a lower rate. I want to see the break-even analysis."

What They Say: "The APR is what really matters for comparison."
What It Really Means: "I'm going to use this technical-sounding number that most people don't understand to distract you from asking about total cost."
Your Response: "I understand APR is one factor. I also need to see total interest paid over the life of the loan, total fees, and total of all payments. That's how I'm comparing."

RED FLAG CATEGORY 3: Pressure and Manipulation Tactics

What They Say: "You're pre-approved for up to $450,000!"
What It Really Means: "The bank will let you borrow way more than you can comfortably afford, and I get paid more on a bigger loan."
Your Response: "What I'm pre-approved for and what I'm comfortable paying are two different things. My comfortable max payment is $[X],XXX per month, which works out to roughly a $[XXX],XXX loan. Let's work with that number."

What They Say: "You need to use our preferred title company."
What It Really Means: "We have a kickback relationship with this title company and they'll overcharge you while giving us referrals or other compensation."
Your Response: "Under RESPA, I have the right to choose my own title company. I'll be getting quotes from at least two other companies. If yours is competitive, I'll consider it."

What They Say: "Shopping around will hurt your credit score."
What It Really Means: "I don't want you talking to my competitors because they might offer you a better deal."
Your Response: "Actually, multiple mortgage inquiries within 45 days count as a single inquiry for credit scoring purposes. I'll be shopping aggressively and my credit will be fine."

What They Say: "Let me run your credit real quick so I can give you an accurate quote."
What It Really Means: "Once I have your credit report, you're in my system and I can pressure you more effectively. Plus, you might feel committed since I 'did work' for you."
Your Response: "I have my credit scores from myFICO.com. Use those for your initial quote. I'll authorize a credit pull only when I'm ready to formally apply with my chosen lender."

What They Say: "I need an application fee to get started."
What It Really Means: "I want your money upfront so you feel committed and are less likely to walk away when I change the terms later."
Your Response: "I don't pay application fees before seeing a written rate lock confirmation. Lock my rate and fees in writing, then I'll pay to proceed."

What They Say: "This is a really competitive rate for someone with your credit score."
What It Really Means: "I'm hoping you don't know what rate you actually qualify for, so you'll accept my marked-up rate as 'competitive.'"
Your Response: "I've researched current rates for my credit score and scenario. The national average for my profile is [X.XX]%. You're quoting [X.XX]%. Explain the difference."

RED FLAG CATEGORY 4: Expertise and Authority Claims

What They Say: "I've been doing this for 20 years, trust me."
What It Really Means: "I've been overcharging people for 20 years and I'm very good at it."

Your Response: "I appreciate your experience. Now show me the documentation: par rate, rate sheet, total compensation, and everything else I've asked for. Experience should make you more comfortable with transparency, not less."

What They Say: "The paperwork is too complicated to explain."
What It Really Means: "I don't want to explain it because the explanation would reveal I'm overcharging you."
Your Response: "I'm capable of understanding financial documents. Walk me through it line by line, or I'll find someone who will."

What They Say: "That's not how the industry works anymore."
What It Really Means: "I was hoping you didn't know how the industry actually works."
Your Response: "Then explain exactly how it works, with documentation. If par rates, rate sheets, and lender paid compensation don't exist anymore, what replaced them?"

What They Say: "You're my only client who's ever asked about this."
What It Really Means: "I'm trying to make you feel like you're being unreasonable or difficult for asking basic questions."
Your Response: "Then I'm your only educated client. Answer my questions or I'll work with someone who appreciates informed borrowers."

What They Say: "Your realtor recommended me, so you know I'm trustworthy."
What It Really Means: "I have a referral relationship with your realtor that may involve kickbacks or reciprocal business arrangements."
Your Response: "I appreciate the referral, but I'm shopping with at least three lenders regardless of who recommended them. If

you're the best option, you'll earn my business through transparency and pricing."

What They Say: "We're a veteran-owned company, so you know we take care of vets."
What It Really Means: "I'm using your service as emotional manipulation to prevent you from asking hard questions."
Your Response: "I respect your service and I'm glad you're using your VA benefit. Now show me you're giving me the same fair treatment by answering all seven questions honestly."

RED FLAG CATEGORY 5: Post-Lock Bait-and-Switch

What They Say: "The underwriter requires a rate increase due to property type."
What It Really Means: "I'm changing the rate I promised you and blaming it on underwriting."
Your Response: "My rate lock confirmation from [date] guarantees [X.XXX]% with no conditions except for changes to my credit or employment. The property type hasn't changed. Honor the locked rate or I'm walking and filing complaints with CFPB and your state regulator."

What They Say: "I have some good news and bad news about your rate..."
What It Really Means: "I'm about to tell you the rate increased, but I'm going to frame it in a way that makes it sound like not that big a deal."
Your Response: "Stop. Pull out my rate lock confirmation. What does it say? That's the rate I'm getting. If you can't honor it, this closing is cancelled."

What They Say: "Your Closing Disclosure shows a slightly different rate than we discussed because the market changed."
What It Really Means: "I'm hoping you won't notice the rate increase or won't push back because you're three days from closing."
Your Response: "My rate is locked per our written agreement dated [XX/XX/XXXX]. The market is irrelevant. Correct the Closing Disclosure immediately or we're not closing."

What They Say: "We found a few additional fees that need to be added."
What It Really Means: "I'm sneaking in extra charges at the last minute when you're too committed to walk away easily."
Your Response: "These fees were not on my Loan Estimate. Either remove them or provide written documentation of what changed in my scenario to justify them. Otherwise I'm not signing."

What They Say: "Can you bring an extra $2,500 to closing? We had some calculation errors."
What It Really Means: "We're trying to extract additional money from you at the last possible moment."
Your Response: "The Closing Disclosure I received three days ago showed my cash to close as $[XXX],XXX. That's what I'm bringing. If your calculations were wrong, that's your problem, not mine."

RED FLAG CATEGORY 6: Defensive Reactions

What They Say: "You're being really difficult about this."
What It Really Means: "You're asking questions I don't want to answer."

Your Response: "Asking for transparency isn't difficult. It's standard for educated borrowers. If you find my questions difficult, I'll work with someone who doesn't."

What They Say: "Do you want this house or not?"
What It Really Means: "I'm using your emotional investment in the property to pressure you into accepting bad terms."
Your Response: "I want the house at fair terms. If you can't provide that, I'll find a lender who can. The house isn't going anywhere in the next 48 hours while I get competing quotes."

What They Say: "Fine, if you don't trust me, go ahead and shop around."
What It Really Means: "I'm calling your bluff because most people back down when confronted with confrontation."
Your Response: "Great, I will. Thanks for your time." [Then actually shop around]

What They Say: "I'm doing you a favor by even giving you a loan with that credit score."
What It Really Means: "I'm trying to make you feel grateful and less likely to negotiate."
Your Response: "My credit score is [XXX], which qualifies me for standard pricing. If you're not comfortable with that score, I'll find a lender who is. No favors necessary."

What They Say: "Other clients never ask these questions."
What It Really Means: "Other clients are easier to rip off."
Your Response: "Then you should be happy to have a client who asks good questions. It makes for a better long-term relationship. Answer them."

What They Say: "You sound like you've been reading too much on the internet."

What It Really Means: "I liked you better when you were ignorant."
Your Response: "I've educated myself because this is the biggest financial transaction of my life. Answer my questions based on facts, not on how much internet research you think I've done."

CRITICAL RULE: If you hear THREE OR MORE of these red flags, WALK AWAY IMMEDIATELY.

The loan officer is either:
1. Deliberately predatory
2. Poorly trained and incompetent
3. Working for a predatory company

None of these scenarios ends well for you. Find a different lender.

APPENDIX D: STATE-BY-STATE INFO

Each state has specific resources for mortgage complaints, consumer protection, and housing assistance. Below are the primary contacts for regulatory oversight and consumer help.

HOW TO USE THIS RESOURCE:
1. Find your state below
2. Contact the State Banking Regulator for licensing verification and complaints
3. Use HUD Housing Counseling for free, independent mortgage advice
4. File complaints with CFPB if lender violates federal law

FEDERAL RESOURCES (All States)

Consumer Financial Protection Bureau (CFPB)

Website: consumerfinance.gov/complaint
Phone: 1-855-411-2372
Handles: Federal mortgage regulation violations, predatory lending, unfair practices

HUD Housing Counseling
Website: hud.gov/program_offices/housing/sfh/hcc
Phone: 1-800-569-4287
Handles: Free housing counseling, foreclosure prevention, homebuying education

NMLS Consumer Access
Website: nmlsconsumeraccess.org
Handles: Loan officer and company license verification, complaint filing

VA Home Loans (Veterans)
Website: benefits.va.gov/homeloans
Phone: 1-877-827-3702
Handles: VA loan complaints, lender certification issues

FHA Resource Center
Website: hud.gov/program_offices/housing/fharesourcectr
Phone: 1-800-767-7468
Handles: FHA loan complaints, approved lender issues

STATE RESOURCES (All 50 States)

Note: Due to space constraints, I'm providing a representative sample. The complete list with all 50 states is available at KeepTheCash.com/resources

ALABAMA
Banking Regulator: Alabama State Banking Department
Website: banking.alabama.gov | Phone: (334) 242-3452

CALIFORNIA
Banking Regulator: CA Dept of Financial Protection and Innovation
Website: dfpi.ca.gov | Phone: (866) 275-2677

FLORIDA
Banking Regulator: Florida Office of Financial Regulation
Website: flofr.gov | Phone: (850) 487-9687

GEORGIA
Banking Regulator: GA Dept of Banking and Finance
Website: dbf.georgia.gov | Phone: (770) 986-1633

ILLINOIS
Banking Regulator: IL Dept of Financial and Professional Regulation
Website: idfpr.com | Phone: (312) 793-3000

NEW YORK
Banking Regulator: NY Department of Financial Services
Website: dfs.ny.gov | Phone: (800) 342-3736

TENNESSEE
Banking Regulator: TN Department of Financial Institutions
Website: tn.gov/tdfi | Phone: (615) 741-2236

TEXAS
Banking Regulator: TX Dept of Savings and Mortgage Lending
Website: sml.texas.gov | Phone: (877) 276-5550

VIRGINIA
Banking Regulator: VA Bureau of Financial Institutions
Website: scc.virginia.gov/bfi | Phone: (804) 371-9657

WASHINGTON
Banking Regulator: WA Department of Financial Institutions
Website: dfi.wa.gov | Phone: (877) 746-4334

For complete state-by-state contact information for all 50 states, visit KeepTheCash.com/state-resources

REMEMBER:
Always start with your state regulator for loan officer licensing verification
File federal complaints with CFPB for violations of federal mortgage laws
Use HUD counseling for free, unbiased mortgage advice
Check NMLS Consumer Access to verify your loan officer's license is current and check for disciplinary actions

Don't let state lines stop you from reporting predatory practices. These regulators work together to track problem lenders and protect consumers nationwide.

WORKS CITED

Clear, James. Atomic Habits: An Easy & Proven Way to Build Good Habits & Break Bad Ones. New York: Avery, 2018.

Covey, Stephen R. The 7 Habits of Highly Effective People: Powerful Lessons in Personal Change. New York: Free Press, 1989.

Ferriss, Timothy. The 4-Hour Workweek: Escape 9-5, Live Anywhere, and Join the New Rich. New York: Crown Publishers, 2007.

Gladwell, Malcolm. Talking to Strangers: What We Should Know About the People We Don't Know. New York: Little, Brown and Company, 2019.

Gladwell, Malcolm. The Tipping Point: How Little Things Can Make a Big Difference. New York: Little, Brown and Company, 2000.

Godin, Seth. Purple Cow: Transform Your Business by Being Remarkable. New York: Portfolio, 2003.

Grant, Adam. Think Again: The Power of Knowing What You Don't Know. New York: Viking, 2021.

Kiyosaki, Robert T. Rich Dad Poor Dad: What the Rich Teach Their Kids About Money That the Poor and Middle Class Do Not! Scottsdale, AZ: Plata Publishing, 1997.

Lewis, Michael. The Big Short: Inside the Doomsday Machine. New York: W. W. Norton & Company, 2010.

Voss, Chris. Never Split the Difference: Negotiating As If Your Life Depended On It. New York: Harper Business, 2016.

FINAL WORD

Look, I've spent the last 100+ pages showing you how the mortgage industry works, where the money goes, and how to protect yourself. But here's what matters most: you now have a choice. You can walk into the mortgage process armed with knowledge, or you can go in blind and hope for the best. Hope is not a strategy, and the industry is counting on you to stay confused.

Do your research. Ask the hard questions. Find a loan officer who doesn't flinch when you ask to see the par rate or the rate sheet. Find someone who welcomes transparency instead of hiding behind industry jargon and "proprietary information" excuses. The smoke and mirrors act that the industry teaches only works on people who don't know the tricks. You know them now. Use that knowledge. The right loan officer will respect you more for asking tough questions, not less. And if they don't respect you for being informed, they don't deserve your business.

I've got twelve kids, and every single one of them is going to get this advice before they buy their first home. I'm not going to let them walk into a closing table and lose $40,000 or $50,000 because some loan officer saw an easy mark. This book is the same advice I'm giving them, and I'm giving it to you for the same reason: because the biggest financial transaction of your life deserves better than blind trust in a broken system.

If you want more straight talk about money, parenting, and navigating life's biggest decisions without getting ripped off, follow me at @DadWith12Kids. I'll keep telling you the truth, even when it makes people uncomfortable. That's what dads do.

Now go keep your cash.

Made in the USA
Monee, IL
04 November 2026

67380796R00066